MEDWAY
QUEEN

RICHARD HALTON

Jointly published by

THE MEDWAY QUEEN PRESERVATION SOCIETY

&

NOODLE **N.B.** *BOOKS*

This edition kindly supported by
The Worshipful Company of Grocers

© Richard Halton & Noodle Books (Kevin Robertson) 2013 & 2014

ISBN 978-1-909328-08-2

First published in 2013, reprinted 2014

A joint production between The Medway Queen Preservation Society and Noodle Books.

www.medwayqueen.co.uk

Medway Queen Project Office
Gillingham Pier
Western Arm
Pier Approach Road
Gillingham, Kent.
ME7 1RX

+44 (0) 1634 575717

The New Medway Steam Packet Company (Medway Queen Preservation Society)
is a Charity. No. 296236. Registered Company No. 2100358

NOODLE BOOKS PO Box 279, Corhampton, SOUTHAMPTON. SO32 3ZX

www.noodlebooks.co.uk

Printed in England by The Information Press.

Every effort has been made to correctly identify and credit material used. If an error has occurred this is entirely unintentional. All unaccredited material is from the MQPS archive or author's private collection.

Front Cover - *Medway Queen dressed overall from a painting by Harley Crossley.*

Title page - *Medway Queen from a drawing by K.C. Lockwood.*

Page 3 - *Medway Queen on her speed trials in 1924.*

Rear cover image - *Medway Queen's engine being installed, Bristol 2012. Bob Sykes.*

CONTENTS

1
DESIGN and BUILD

From the minutes of a board meeting of the New Medway Steam Packet Company on October 8th 1923:

"Resolved that a new boat be ordered at a cost not exceeding £21,500 that the contract be given to the Ailsa Shipbuilding Co. Ltd. of Troon, subject to an approved specification & plan of detail be submitted for the board's approval."

The Medway Steam Packet Company was originally formed in 1837. It provided steamer services in the Chatham - Sheerness area into the early 1880s. The company was reconstituted in 1881 and gradually built up a fleet of ships, in due course replacing the older vessels. By the beginning of the First World War the company ran two ships on a regular service between Strood and Southend-on-Sea. At the start of that war their paddle steamers City of Rochester and Princess of Wales were requisitioned for naval duties and the service ceased. In 1919 the company was reformed as the New Medway Steam Packet Company Ltd. with Captain Sydney J. Shippick as Managing Director and once more began services in the Medway area. The new company expanded quickly and two further ships were added to the fleet; PS Audrey and PS Queen of the South. Both were purchased second hand.

In 1923 it was decided to build a further ship and the contract for the construction of Medway Queen was awarded to the Ailsa Ship Building Company of Troon. The new ship was to be ready for the 1924 season. Ailsa was one of the smaller yards on the Clyde but one with a good reputation and a history of building paddle steamers. With a budget of £21,500 approved (equivalent to about £1M today) one wonders what the gentlemen of the board would have made of the restoration costs in the region of £5M at the beginning of the 21st century!

During the First World War Ailsa had designed the famous "Racecourse" class of paddle minesweepers and had built 3 of them. They also built the first two vessels of an improved variant. Other ships of the class were built elsewhere and two of them later became the New Medway Company's PS Queen of Kent and PS Queen of Thanet. Another, HMS Ascot, was the very first built (also by Ailsa) and had the dubious distinction of being the last warship sunk in the First World War when she was torpedoed by UB-67 on 10th November 1918.

Medway Queen was constructed using the traditional plate on frame technique. The frames were built up first using the keel structure as a base. These frames are generally constructed of 3" x 3"x 3/16" angle iron but are of heavier section towards the ship's bottom

The hull plating was fixed in place plate by plate, with butt straps used to join the plates in horizontal strips and those strips overlapped and riveted to make the horizontal joints. The majority of the plate is only ¼inch (6mm) thickness, but in some places, notably around the keel and ships bottom and on the sheer-strake heavier plate is used, some being 5/16inch (8mm) and some 3/8 inch (10mm). Lighter plating was also used, 3/16 inch (5mm) in certain places and above the main deck 5/32inch (4mm) plate is generally used.

Left - Medway Queen was launched on Wednesday April 23rd (St George's Day) 1924 by Mrs. C. Willis, wife of the company chairman.

The internal joints on bulkheads etc., were assembled using conventional round head rivets. The hull plating is flush riveted to reduce drag when the ship moves through the water. This requires the rivets to be countersunk on the outer surface. The traditional way of doing this is to insert a standard rivet from the inside of the hull and to form a countersunk head into a tapered recess on the outside plating. The countersink recess has to be properly filled by the deformed metal to produce a good strong joint without voids.

Medway Queen
Technical Specification

Yard Number: P.S.388
UK Official Number 148361
Tonnage: 316grt (134 net)
Length: 180feet (54.9m)
Beam: 24feet (7.3m)
Width over paddle frame: 50ft (15.2m)
Normal Draft: 5feet 6inches (1.7m)
Cruising Speed: 13knots at 45rpm
Max Speed: 15knots at 55rpm
Construction: Steel plate riveted on frames
Engine: Compound diagonal
Boiler: Scotch type 11ft (3.4m) long
Coal fired with triple furnaces.

Medway Queen's main engine was also constructed by Ailsa. It is a compound diagonal steam engine. That is to say there are two cylinders working at different steam pressure. Steam goes first into the smaller, high pressure, cylinder and then into the larger, low pressure, one while it is still expanding. The "diagonal" reference indicates to the alignment of the cylinders. "Horizontal" and "vertical" are self explanatory in this context; "diagonal" is between the two and ensures that the thrust or power is directed downward onto the strongest part of the hull.

The quality of work produced by the Ailsa Shipbuilding Company was such that some eighty five years later when the ship was being rebuilt in Bristol the restorers were impressed by the ease with which some parts and joints could be renewed. Fittings that had been in use for years and then spent many more years immersed in salty mud were persuaded to come apart with far less effort than had been expected.

During her working life, a number of modifications were made to Medway Queen's specification. A bow rudder was fitted in 1936 to aid manoeuvering in harbour and the ship was converted to oil firing in 1938 At the start of the Second World War, and again at the end, substantial re-building took place to adapt her to new roles.

Medway Queen was launched with due ceremony on Wednesday 23rd April 1924. The naming was performed by Mrs. C. Willis, wife of the company Chairman in the presence of invited guests and the directors of both Ailsa and of the New Medway Steam Packet Company. Fitting out followed and eventually commissioning of her engines and other machinery. Sea trials took place in the Firth of Clyde and the ship met all the expectations of her proud owners.

The delivery run was undertaken without incident although a rousing reception and enticements to moor were observed while passing Bournemouth and Southend. Medway Queen arrived at her new home on the river Medway on 10th July 1924. The local paper reported the event the following day: "The Medway Queen has arrived! In glorious sunshine and before the expectant eyes of throngs of people lining the end of Sun Pier the handsome vessel resplendent in glittering brass-work and varnish and arrayed in gay bunting dropped anchor off the pier shortly before 2.30pm yesterday."

The engineer responsible for that delivery, Mr. Thomas Hunter Rickson Wilson, was so taken with Rochester that he decided to re-locate there with his family. Some years later his son, George Barclay Wilson, joined the Royal Army Service Corps and in 1940 found himself in France driving a lorry towards Dunkirk On arrival he was told to ruin the engine and head for the beach where he joined thousands of others waiting to be picked up. He boarded the Crested Eagle from the East Mole just as a bomb hit the ship but was lucky enough to get back on the Mole. He then boarded Medway Queen (his Dad's old ship) and was taken back to Britain.

The upper saloons were fitted with wide windows so that passengers could get a good view of what was going on around them while they dined. In the lower saloons, round portholes were fitted just above the water line. These would admit light but provided a very restricted view out. The lower saloons were fitted out as bars while the upper saloons were fitted for restaurant and tea shop use. The management had the presence of mind to arrange a tour for the "News" reporter who was very taken with the "sumptuously upholstered saloons, each fitted with tea and refreshment bars and toilet accommodation for both males and females with white and silver fittings"

Opposite top - Engine Room. R W Wright.
Opposite lower left - George Barclay Wilson. Courtesy Mrs Barbara Luscombe.
Opposite lower right - Thomas Hunter Rickson Wilson. Courtesy Mrs Barbara Luscombe.

Medway Queen shortly before entering service.

Medway Queen's maiden voyage was in the form of a shake-down cruise for invited guests and dignitaries. This took place on Friday 18th July 1924 and the first guests boarded at Strood. They included the Mayor and Mayoress of Rochester, Captain J. H. Wills of the General Steam Navigation Company Ltd. and his wife, Mr. A.S. Arnold, the Chief Constable and numerous Councilors and Aldermen. Company management was well represented and included Captain Shippick, Councilor E. Scones (Company Secretary) and Mr. C. Willis (Chairman). They departed at about 10.05am and moved down river as the previously threatening clouds gave way to sunshine.

The first port of call was Sun Pier, Chatham, where the Mayor of Chatham and numerous other dignitaries came aboard. Also among the guests here was Mr. Alex Campbell of P & A Campbell Ltd., Bristol. The journey continued and observation of a shoal of porpoises added further excitement to the day. A stop to pick up a single guest was made at Sheerness, after which the ship set sail for Southend arriving at 11.30. Her arrival was greeted by a salvo of rockets launched from the pier and a welcoming crowd of holiday makers. Another civic deputation was taken on board and despite warnings of choppy conditions at Herne Bay the journey continued to that destination.

Medway Queen and her crew quickly settled in to providing a regular shuttle service across the Thames Estuary between Chatham and the other Medway towns to Southend. Captain T. J (Tommy) Aldis was given command of Medway Queen for her first two seasons, after which he moved to Queen of Thanet. Leonard Horsham (later to command Medway Queen) was his first officer. There might be 2 or even 3 return trips a day from Chatham or Strood across to Southend, timed and advertised to maximise the time ashore for day trippers.

Under the guidance of Captain Shippick, the New Medway fleet expanded considerably in the 1920s. Three

vessels from the Belle Steamers fleet were acquired between 1924 and 1928. The Woolwich Belle, Walton Belle and Yarmouth Belle were named Queen of the South, Essex Queen and Queen of Southend. This last was later renamed Thames Queen.

Two "Racecourse" class paddle minesweepers were also purchased. HMS Atherstone was built by Ailsa SB and was launched on 14 April 1916. She served with the "Auxiliary Patrol" and later worked with the Mine Clearance Service. She was sold to The New Medway Steam Packet Company on 12 August 1927 and converted for excursion work. She was renamed Queen of Kent.

Navy Week postcard.

P. S. MEDWAY QUEEN.   Copyright Photo.

NMSPC postcard.

HMS Melton was built by William Hamilton and Co. of Port Glasgow and was launched in March 1916. She too served for the rest of the war with the Auxiliary Patrol, At the end of the war she was transferred to the Mine Clearance Service.

HMS Melton had been sold to Hughes Bolckow Shipbreaking Co in 1927. She was bought by The New Medway Steam Packet Company in 1929 and converted for excursion work on the Thames and Medway rivers. She was renamed Queen of Thanet and over the next twelve years both ships worked between Sheerness and Southend. Excursion work and scheduled services also took them further afield including cross-channel voyages to Calais, Dunkirk and Boulogne.

On Medway Queen Captain Aldis was succeeded by Captain Bob Hayman for the 1926 season and he then remained in command until the outbreak of war. Special events and planned excursions added to the variety of what was otherwise a regular shuttle service across the Thames estuary. Naval comings and goings and events such as "Navy Week" at Chatham Dockyard all added to the mix. The illustrations include a Medway Queen postcard which carries an inscription referring to Chatham Navy Week in 1934. Postcards such as this

were, presumably, sold on board. Chatham dockyard and Royal Navy ships moored in the river would be points of interest on any trip and often there were passengers who worked in the dockyard and would point out their places of work or the ships they had been working on. The company's steamer services were operated during the summer only with the ships being laid up from mid-September until around the end of May. The Whitsun holiday weekend was a favourite start date for the new season.

A flavour of the crew's daily routine in pre-war days can be had through an account left by Mr. Ernie Crittenden of his experiences as a galley boy in 1936. This first appeared in the MQPS society's magazine in the early days of the society.

"I worked as a galley boy at the age of 14 years in what, for me, was a happy and exciting experience. The hours were long (average 14) and my wage was 12/5d (62 ½ p) per week. Time did not matter in those days and although legally a juvenile was not permitted such long hours there was no point on our journey where I could be put off when my legal hours had been reached.

The day began with the loading of crates of beer and

Left - *Medway Queen at Gillingham. War and Peace collection.*

A pre-war view of Medway Queen. E Cole.

foodstuffs and one learned to keep an eye on the tide. The tide would determine the angle at which the gangplank was pitched for loading the stores. As you can imagine, a steep gangplank was not very popular and at times was decidedly "hairy".

Our galley range, which was a coal burner, shared the main smoke stack and it was not uncommon for a blow back of smoke which often left the chef and me choking. I was given urgent orders to run on deck and alter the direction of the vent cowls to hasten the removal of the smoke. The chef at the time was Mr. Tom Hester and I was firmly convinced that he could perform miracles with food. The varied jars and tins from which he produced "magic" powders held me in awe and I sampled flavours that I had never tasted before or since. The skipper (Captain Hayman) always congratulated him on providing a fine meal and so did many others!

My daily tasks, apart from helping with the loading and unloading of stores etc., were numerous. Scrubbing the floor was not among my favourite tasks because it was composed of small tiles with grooves which required a lot of elbow grease to get them clean. The tiny drainage hole in the floor was also a constant nuisance as it was always getting blocked. However, the rest of my duties made up for any displeasure that I might have. On my first day I

was asked to fill a huge oval cast iron saucepan. It was as much as I could do to lift it empty. I placed it adjacent to the sink and filled it with a small pot which seemed to take ages. When I announced that the saucepan was full I was asked how I expected to get it across to the range. I had not thought of that! – When my blushes had subsided I proceeded to empty some of the water by baling it into the sink. This brought another rebuke and I was told that the water was carried in storage tanks and I must go easy with its use. Later that day I learned that it was my job to pump water by hand from a lower reserve tank to the upper main tank. This operation entailed lying down on the deck and reaching under a seat for the pump handle and often meant having to ask a passenger to move."

Mr. Crittenden also remembered other incidents on board from his time on the ship:

"We had picked up a large number of trippers from Southend, mainly Londoners, and were making for Herne Bay when we grounded on a sandbank at low tide. I watched from the paddle box rail the effort to get the "Queen" free and remember vividly the sand being churned up by the paddle blades. In the end, we had to wait for the tide to lift us off. This incident was mentioned in the "News of the World" which stated that hardly a passenger was aware of the grounding. I can believe this *as a good old "knees up" was going on above and had been since we cast off from Southend. On another occasion the "Queen" hit a submerged wreck which snapped one of the rods attached to a paddle blade. With no support at one end of the blade the free end struck the top of the paddle box a few times before the engine was stopped. Then began the long task of sawing through the rod to release the paddle blade. The blade had to be salvaged, so some crew members had to sit on the paddle in the water to support it while other crew members took it in turns in using the hacksaw on the rod. The blade was eventually released and re-fitted soon after."*

"I wonder how many people realised that the "Queen" was no stranger to the role of troopship. This was during the season of 1936 when we were told that we were to take 800 soldiers to Felixstowe, I was to remain on board overnight for an early call at 1am in order to peel 2cwt (about 102kgm) of potatoes by 10.30am. Whoever did the estimating was very good. I just managed it but no longer have the blisters to prove it. After this marathon I was not happy to see much of the food the chef and I had prepared being deposited over the side and on deck by some unfortunates who were suffering from sea-sickness."

He remembered too that there were more sombre moments such as the sudden collapse and death of the purser in the forward saloon.

In a further expansion in the late 1930s, the company invested in three new Motor Vessels. These were MV Royal Daffodil, MV Queen of the Channel and MV

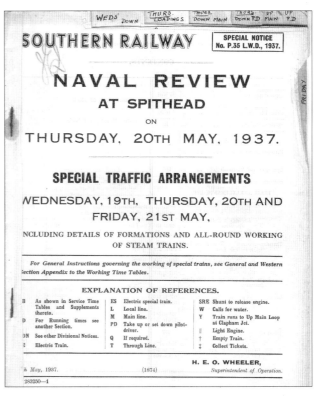

Royal Sovereign. The original Royal Daffodil was a steam ship from the river Mersey which had gained the "Royal" prefix in recognition of her part in the Zeebrugge raid during the First World War. The New Medway Company had bought her in 1934. When she was scrapped in 1938 the name was used for the new Motor Vessel built by William Deny Bros of Dumbarton. MV Queen of the Channel was also built by William

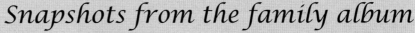

Wish you were here!

Snapshots from the family album

With thanks to Charles Hewett and Mr H Anderson.

MEDWAY QUEEN

New Medway Steam Packet Company, Ltd.

Wine List & Tariff

SEASON 1927.

STEAMERS:
'ESSEX QUEEN' 'QUEEN OF THE SOUTH'
'MEDWAY QUEEN' 'CITY OF ROCHESTER'
'AUDREY'

MOTOR LAUNCHES:
'ROCHESTER CITY BELLE'
'NEW MEDWAY' 'H.R.H. PRINCESS MARY'

Registered Office:
280 HIGH ST., ROCHESTER.

Managing Director:
S. J. SHIPPICK.

Denny Bros. The Royal Sovereign was planned as MV Continental Queen, to be owned by a semi-independent company but the General Steam Navigation Company (GSN) bought a majority shareholding in the New Medway Steam Packet Company in 1937 and the ship entered service as MV Royal Sovereign. Although now effectively controlled by the GSN the New Medway fleet continued to operate under their old name up to the Second World War and then again in the 1940s, '50s and into the 1960s.

In 1937 Medway Queen attended the Spithead Naval Review in celebration of the Coronation of King George VI. The ship ran an excursion on the day of the Review for a pre-booked party from London who travelled down by train on the morning of the event and returned to London in the small hours of the next day.

We know from the Southern Railway company's special workings instruction documents that Medway Queen's train was scheduled to leave London Victoria at 0705 on Thursday 20th May 1937 and travel down to Portsmouth and Southsea station, arriving at 0916. There must then have been connecting transport to where the ship was berthed. Portsmouth Harbour Station was not used in this

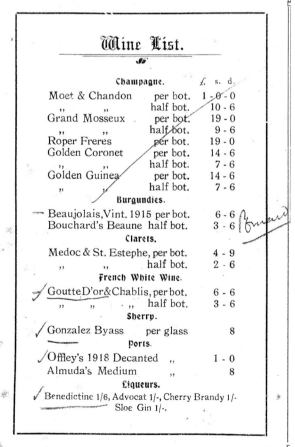

Tariff.

Luncheon.	s.	d.
Hot Cut from Joint, Sweet Biscuit & Cheese	3	0
Cold Meats, Potatoes (Hot) Salad, Biscuits, Cheese, Etc.	2	6
Fruit Salad with Cream ...		8
Meat Tea.		
With Salad, Pickles, etc., and Pot of Tea, inclusive charge	2	0
Plain Tea.		
Pot of Tea, Bread and Butter and Cake or Jam	1	0
Tea per Pot (each Person) ...		4
Bun, or Roll and Butter ...		3
Bread and Butter (per piece)		1½
Fruit Cake (per piece) ...		3
Pastries		2½
Buns		1½
Tea (per cup)		2½
Coffee (per cup)		3
Cocoa (per cup)		3
Bovril		6

Wine List.

Champagne.		£	s.	d.
Moet & Chandon	per bot.	1	0	0
,, ,,	half bot.		10	6
Grand Mosseux	per bot.		19	0
,, ,,	half bot.		9	6
Roper Freres	per bot.		19	0
Golden Coronet	per bot.		14	6
,, ,,	half bot.		7	6
Golden Guinea	per bot.		14	6
,, ,,	half bot.		7	6
Burgundies.				
Beaujolais, Vint. 1915	per bot.		6	6
Bouchard's Beaune	half bot.		3	6
Clarets.				
Medoc & St. Estephe,	per bot.		4	9
,, ,,	half bot.		2	6
French White Wine.				
Goutte D'or & Chablis,	per bot.		6	6
,, ,, ,,	half bot.		3	6
Sherry.				
Gonzalez Byass	per glass			8
Ports.				
Offley's 1918 Decanted	,,		1	0
Almuda's Medium	,,			8
Liqueurs.				
Benedictine 1/6, Advocat 1/-, Cherry Brandy 1/- Sloe Gin 1/-.				

instance. The General Steam Navigation Company hired 3 other trains conveying a total of 1576 passengers for MV Royal Daffodil and a part share in a train with 200 passengers for PS City of Rochester. Medway Queen's train had a capacity of 540 people. Other company ships also took part including MV Queen of the Channel and the paddle steamers Queen of Kent and Queen of Thanet but their trains were hired by other organisations and presumably the vessel's capacity was similarly sub-let. After the event, Medway Queen's passengers left Portsmouth and Southsea station at 02.27 in the morning of Friday 21st May and arrived back in London, Victoria at 04.25.

Sun Pier.   *George Painter collection.*

Sun Pier, in Chatham, was an integral part of the New Medway company services. It had a rigid upper structure with lower level pontoons that rose and fell with the tides. It is now no more than a shadow of the magnificent structure that existed in the Medway Queen's operational life and the following description by George Painter, who has researched the pier's history, is well worth inclusion:
Although the pier is still functioning, it is minus the enormous canopy which was destroyed by fire in the 1960s. Beneath this canopy was the Pier Master's office, ice cream parlour and tea room. There was the familiar Nestles 2d chocolate vending machine but the main attraction was the aluminium strip name printer which was popular with all ages. For 1d a name could be embossed to become a keep-sake forever.

This magnificent structure was a focal point in the centre of Chatham, not only the main terminal for the steamers but also for the grey motor boats which ran a shuttle service to Upnor beach. Families in the 1930s would visit the pier just to enjoy the riverside activity and soak up what was generally a happy atmosphere. These were hard times but if finances allowed there was an ice cream or even a 4d trip on the motor boat to Upnor beach. A trip on a paddle steamer would be part of a main holiday

and would have to be carefully saved for. The Pier Master was always smartly dressed in his uniform and seemed to spend most of his time chasing children with their bent pins and string away from the lower pontoon where they were engrossed in another great pier adventure – Crab Fishing

At the entrance to the pier were two kiosks, situated at either side. For would be passengers on the steamers it depended on the chosen destination as to which kiosk was used. There were sometimes several steamers picking up passengers at one time so there would be a flurry of activity. There was no formal queuing in those pre-war days; passengers would approach the kiosk window in an orderly manner and politely wait their turn. Opposite the pier entrance was the courtyard beer garden of the King's Head public house. This was frequented by returning trippers to complete a perfect day out. The families would sit around the beer-barrel tables; Dad with his pint of Mild ale, Mum with her Mackeson stout and the children with lemonade and Smith's crisps. They had found total contentment!

Mr. W. G. Peake was appointed Engineer Superintendent of the New Medway Steam Packet Co. in 1937 and moved to Rochester. One of his first jobs was to oversee Medway Queen's conversion from coal to oil-firing by the Wallsend Slipway & Engineering Company on Tyneside (part of the Swan Hunter organisation) in 1938. This was to have a profound influence on her later career. During the Dunkirk evacuation she could refuel far more quickly and easily than her coal fired sisters.

On the outbreak of war in 1939 children and some other people were evacuated from the more dangerous areas to places of safety. In some instances this was carried out by sea and on the morning of Friday 1st September Medway Queen and 6 of her consorts from the GSN and New Medway companies queued up to take people from the Ford jetty in Dagenham to East Anglia. Medway Queen sailed to Felixstowe where the children slept in some very temporary accommodation until the next day when they moved on to their final destinations. A repeat performance was held on the following day with the additional assistance of PS Laguna Belle. In all almost 17000 people were moved in this two day operation although exact numbers were not recorded. On the 3rd of September the ships, including Medway Queen, picked up evacuees from the West Pier, Gravesend in Kent, and carried them to Lowestoft. This voyage is remarkable in that 3 more passengers are reported to have landed than had boarded at Gravesend. During the course of the voyage 3 new babies had been born. It is also recorded that some of the newly arrived young evacuees, when asked where they had come from, replied "from

Medway Queen approaching Sun pier, Chatham.

England". They had been out of site of land and were obviously unaware of the exact itinerary of their journey.

Medway Queen was requisitioned by the Admiralty on 9 September for war service as a minesweeper. The paddle steamers Queen of Kent and Queen of Thanet had also been requisitioned by the Admiralty for minesweeping duties. They were commissioned as HMS Queen of Kent, pennant number J74, and HMS Queen of Thanet, pennant number J30. Like Medway Queen, Queen of Thanet took part in the Dunkirk evacuation in 1940 rescuing 4000 men in four trips. The three motor vessels were also taken over and served at Dunkirk where Queen of the Channel was sunk and Royal Daffodil severely damaged.

PROGRAMME of
SUMMER DAY CRUISES
from SOUTHEND PIER

EAGLE AND QUEEN LINE

4th June to September 1938

Commencing 4th JUNE
DAILY except FRIDAYS
(but including Fridays in August)

'MEDWAY QUEEN'
at 11.15 a.m.
for
SHEERNESS
FIVE HOURS ASHORE
CHATHAM
about THREE HOURS ASHORE
ROCHESTER
OVER TWO HOURS ASHORE

FARES

	Single	Day Rt.	Per. Rt.
SHEERNESS	1/6	2/-	2/6
CHATHAM ROCHESTER }	2/-	3/-	4/-

Children up to 14 years—Half Fare

TIMES

SOUTHEND	dep.	11.15 a.m.
SHEERNESS	arr.	11.45 ,,
CHATHAM	,,	12.45 p.m.
STROOD	,,	1.0 ,,
(for Rochester)		
,,	dep.	3.15 ,,
CHATHAM	,,	3.30 ,,
GILLINGHAM	,,	3.45 ,,
SHEERNESS	,,	4.40 ,,
SOUTHEND	arr.	5.15 ,,

Leaves at once for
MEDWAY PIERS

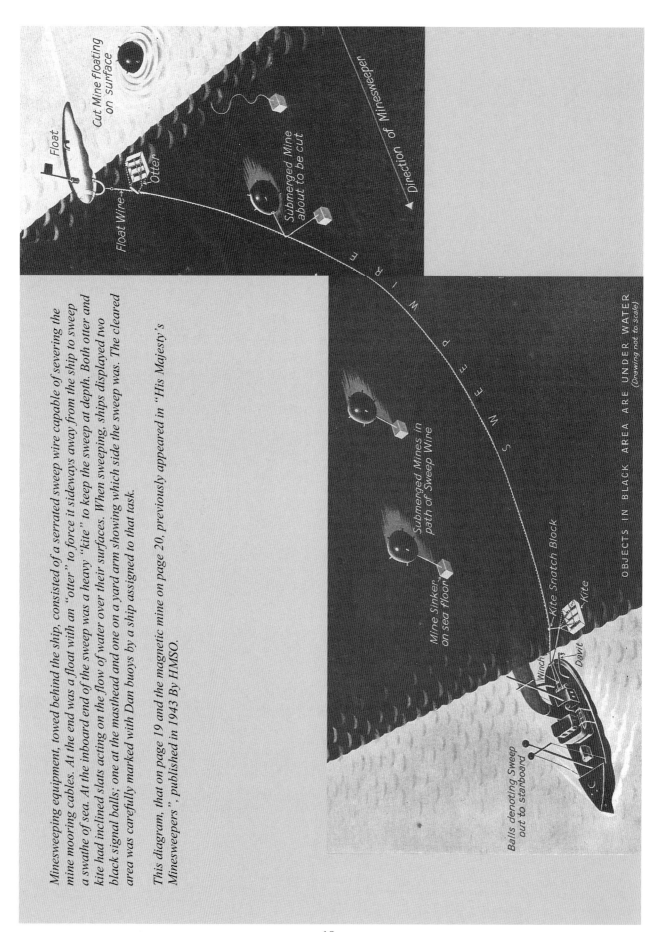

Minesweeping equipment, towed behind the ship, consisted of a serrated sweep wire capable of severing the mine mooring cables. At the end was a float with an "otter" to force it sideways away from the ship to sweep a swathe of sea. At the inboard end of the sweep was a heavy "kite" to keep the sweep at depth. Both otter and kite had inclined slats acting on the flow of water over their surfaces. When sweeping, ships displayed two black signal balls; one at the masthead and one on a yard arm showing which side the sweep was. The cleared area was carefully marked with Dan buoys by a ship assigned to that task.

This diagram, that on page 19 and the magnetic mine on page 20, previously appeared in "His Majesty's Minesweepers", published in 1943 By HMSO.

Cut Mine floating on surface

Float

Float Wire

Otter

Submerged Mine about to be cut

Direction of Minesweeper

SWEEP WIRE

Submerged Mines in path of Sweep Wire

Mine Sinker on sea floor

Kite Snatch Block

Kite

Davit

Winch

Balls denoting Sweep out to starboard

OBJECTS IN BLACK AREA ARE UNDER WATER
(Drawing not to scale)

18

3
MINESWEEPING

At the outbreak of war the Royal Navy had an embryonic fleet of minesweepers and the hard won knowledge from WWI had been retained. Four Halcyon class minesweepers were laid down in 1933 and a total of 21 were completed by 1939. At the start of the war the Admiralty requisitioned many trawlers and other fishing boats to provide the numbers of craft needed. Training programmes were initiated and technical improvements made to equipment. As in WWI converted excursion paddle steamers were used, including Medway Queen.

Medway Queen was converted for minesweeping at the GSN Company's yard in Deptford. She was armed with a 12pdr gun on the fore deck and a machine gun on each paddle box. These are believed to have been Hotchkiss guns initially but they were soon replaced with twin Lewis guns. The upper aft saloon was cut away to provide deck space for the mine sweeping gear. The windows were plated over and peacetime fittings were removed. She was painted grey and given pennant number N48, (later changed to J48). The bridge was enlarged and strengthened and partly covered in. She was commissioned as HMS Medway Queen by her First Lieutenant; Sub-Lieutenant J. D. Graves RNR in November 1939.

During WWII the most common type of mine was the buoyant contact mine. This had a heavy sinker which rested on the sea bottom as an anchor. The mine floated at a pre-determined depth on a long cable and contained an explosive charge which would be fired electrically when a ship struck one of the detonator horns on the casing. The British Mk19 mine of 1940 contained a 100lb charge of TNT.

Mines were used in two ways. Minefields could be laid in pre-planned positions in a defensive barrage or they could also be used offensively to sink or disrupt shipping. The antidote to the contact mine was "sweeping" to clear shipping lanes, using the "Oropesa" Sweep, named after the ship on which the technique was developed in 1919. This equipment, towed behind the ship, consisted of a serrated sweep wire capable of severing the mine mooring cables. At the end was a float with an "otter" to force it sideways away from the ship to sweep a swathe of sea. At the inboard end of the sweep was a heavy "kite" to keep the sweep wire at depth. Both otter and kite had inclined slats acting on the flow of water over their surfaces. Severed mines would float to the surface and were then sunk or exploded by gun fire. When sweeping, ships displayed two black signal balls; one at the masthead and one on a yard arm showing on which side the sweep was deployed. The cleared area was

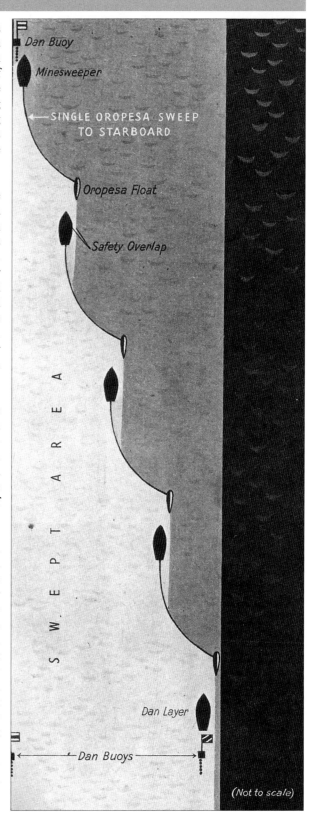

Dan Buoy

Minesweeper

← SINGLE OROPESA SWEEP TO STARBOARD

Oropesa Float

Safety Overlap

S W E P T   A R E A

Dan Layer

← Dan Buoys →

(Not to scale)

HMS Medway Queen at Dover. PSPS Collection

carefully marked with "Dan" marker buoys by a ship assigned to that task.

In 1942 the "Mk 1 Obstructor" was developed. This was a sinker-moored cable with a float, designed to sever the minesweeping wires. The Royal Navy laid these around the edges of some minefields to hamper sweeping.

The principles of magnetic mines were known before the war. The first British magnetic mines were in service in 1942, but the German mines came much earlier and in November 1939 two unexploded examples were discovered ashore near Shoeburyness. One was defused by Lieutenant-commanders Ouvry and Lewis, CPO. Baldwin and AB. Vearncombe of HMS Vernon's Mine Experimental Department. The other was dealt with by Lieutenant J. E. M. Glenny. The mines were taken away for examination at HMS Vernon and all five men were decorated for their bravery.

Magnetic mines detonate when they sense the magnetic field of a ship. The antidote was to negate that field with an opposite field generated by a "de-gaussing" coil wrapped around the hull and energized by a generator. They could be cleared by generating "false" magnetic

The magnetic mine washed ashore at Shoeburyness.

fields with cables between ships or on specially built barges. A squadron of Wellington bombers was equipped with generators and large metal coils which could detonate mines while the aircraft flew low over the sea. All ships were rapidly fitted with de-gaussing coils.

Later in the war sound activated acoustic mines and pressure mines were developed and countermeasures had to be evolved. For acoustic mines the "SA Acoustic Hammer" was developed. Basically it was a pneumatic riveting gun beating on a steel sheet to send out sound waves under water that would detonate the mine ahead of

HMS Medway Queen at Dover. PSPS Collection

the ship. This could be mounted internally inside the bow or externally. An indistinct photograph of Medway Queen in 1941 might show this equipment mounted on the bow but it is not certain.

Medway Queen's captain was Sub-Lieutenant R. D. C. Cooke RNVR. with Sub-Lieutenant Graves as second in command. The navigating officer was Lieutenant Jolly RNVR and the junior officer was Lieutenant Keilly RNR who in theory actually out ranked all the others.

After commissioning, HMS Medway Queen went to Gravesend for gun trials and thence to Chatham for the necessary adjustments. She was booked in through the lock at 0850 on the 21st December, emerging at 1135 on the 8th of January 1940. Medway Queen arrived in Sheerness on 10th January and then proceeded to Harwich where she acted as an independent ship under the direct control of FOIC Harwich. At first they were employed in sweeping the lower part of the Thames estuary for contact mines. The winter of 1939 was bitterly cold and ice formed even on those tidal waters. This presented a serious danger to the paddles and at times a tug was required to act as ice breaker. Medway Queen returned to Chatham in late January. She was booked in through the dockyard lock for maintenance at 0915 on 29th February until 0940 on 7th March. It must have been during one of her two visits to Chatham Dockyard that she acquired her distinctive derrick at the stern for handling the minesweeping apparatus. This was reckoned to be more efficient than the usual boat davit but the idea was not generally taken up by other ships. The modification was unofficial and it is rumoured that it cost the ship a case of whisky. De-gaussing protection against magnetic mines

appears to have been fitted on the second visit, but on a more official basis.

Medway Queen and her crew then joined the 10th minesweeping flotilla, based in Dover under the command of Commander K. M. Greig RN in HMS Sandown. At some time in the spring of 1940 Medway Queen's captain retired for health reasons and Lieutenant A.T. Cook RNR took command. The flotilla consisted of 8 ships, all paddle mine sweepers:

DUCHESS OF ROTHESAY (Lt J Dixon RNVR)
BRIGHTON BELLE (Lt L.K. Perrin RNVR)
EMPEROR OF INDIA (Lt Cdr B. R. Booth RNR)
GRACIE FIELDS (Lt. N. Larkin RNR)
MEDWAY QUEEN (Lt A. T. Cook RNR)
PRINCESS ELIZABETH (Lt W. D. King RNR)
RYDE (Lt J G Allen RNR)
SANDOWN (Cdr K. M. Greig DSO Retired, Acting)

The 10th flotilla took a very active part in Operation Dynamo, the evacuation from Dunkirk, which is described in the next chapter. Several of the flotilla's ships were damaged and two had been sunk. Most of the flotilla was sent to Portsmouth for repairs and by Wednesday 19th June 1940 the 10th Mine Sweeping Flotilla, now composed of just two active ships, HMS Medway Queen and HMS Princess Elizabeth, arrived back at Dover to rejoin HMS Ryde. Two more ships of the Flotilla were expected to join shortly when their refitting was completed. By late June the 10th Minesweeping Flotilla was regaining its strength. HMS Duchess of Rothsay was still at Southampton under

Watching the sweeps. PSPS Collection.

repair but the other ships had returned to duty at Dover as their repairs were completed.

In July the 10th moved to Yarmouth from where they continued their mine clearance work. In August 1940, Medway Queen was transferred to the 8th Minesweeping Flotilla at North Shields on the river Tyne. The flotilla was made up of eight paddle minesweepers:

GLEN AVON (Lt Cdr A. Stubbs RNR)
GLEN GOWER (SO, Acting Cdr M. A. O. Biddulph)
GLEN USK (Lt Cdr N. F. Wills RNVR),
LAGUNA BELLE (Lt Cdr A. O. Foden RNR)
MEDWAY QUEEN (Lt A. T. Cook DSC RNR),
SNAEFELL (Lt Cdr F. Brett RNR)
SOUTHSEA (Lt Cdr C. C. M. Pawley RNR)
THAMES QUEEN (Lt Cdr J. Martin-Smith DSC RNR)

A few log books survive from the latter part of 1940 and they tell of a routine that went on day after day with little excitement aside from air-raid "Red Alarms" when the machine guns were closed up. The hands would be called at 0600 and they would leave harbour at about 0730. The crew's breakfast was at 0800. and they would start sweeping at about that same time. "Up Spirits" was at 1100 and hands to dinner at 1200. The watchmen would eat prior to that. They might return to base around 1430 and then if necessary refuel at the Jarrow Oil Jetty. This would take a couple of hours or so. "Darken Ship" was at 1930, liberty men aboard by 2000 and Rounds Complete at 2100. Pipe Down was at 2200.

The routine would be broken for maintenance and periodic boiler cleaning. For example on Thursday 7th November 1940 the ship went in for a boiler clean and some unspecified maintenance:

> 0630 Called Hands
> 0645 Pumped forepeak
> 0730 Called Officers
> 0900 Colours
> 0930 Tug alongside, let go buoys
> 1000 Secured alongside Laguna Belle
>   in the Albert Edward Dock
> 1415 Hands for payment
> 1600 Ships company proceed on leave

The men returned on Friday 15th November and the normal routine started again on the following day.

MINESWEEPING

Out Sweeps!

PS Southsea had been built in 1930 by Fairfield Govan for the Southern Railway Company for the ferry service to the Isle of Wight. She became HMS Southsea early in 1940 and was assigned to the 8th flotilla. On 16th February 1941 she was following Medway Queen back to base and as they passed North Tyne Pier Light she was damaged by a mine. It was probably an acoustic mine which Medway Queen had passed safely but Southsea did not. Either Medway Queen had not been in range or the mine allowed several ships to pass before detonating. HMS Southsea was beached near South Shields but Lt (E) G M Barnes RNR, Sub Lt P Pawsey RNVR and five ratings were lost. She was found to be beyond reasonable repair and declared a total loss.

Albert Skinner, who had served on Medway Queen since before Dunkirk, was awarded the Royal Humane Society's certificate for saving a seaman who fell overboard. Mr. Skinner has left an account of what happened. *"I had been ashore and had to get back early to be on watch on the gangway at 8pm. At about 10pm when the pubs shut, I heard a few fellows coming along, singing and laughing, and returning on board. I heard a splash and a shout of Man Overboard. I dropped my rifle and ran down the gangway, kicking my sea boots off as I ran for'ard. I went over the side where our Jacob's ladder was, which was used for tying up to the buoy and held up the man who had gone overboard while I hung on to the bottom of the ladder with my arm. He was well boozed. I called up our First Lieutenant and others who were on deck and shining torches down. I thought I would have to get a bowline round him as they could not send a boat to us because a ship was tied up alongside us and ours was inboard. The other vessel's boat was away.*

The man I was trying to assist was getting a bit weighty by now as he had on his overcoat and sea boots, and also

carried his gas mask, but he seemed to have sobered up through the immersion. He was beginning to recover and said he felt all right now and could climb up the ladder himself. I got his two hands firmly on the rung and climbed the ladder myself when - splash - and I'm bothered if he hadn't got up a couple of rungs and then let go, so I had to adopt the same procedure all over again. I called up to the effect that we would have to get a bowline round him somehow when just at that moment our 1st Lieutenant called down to me to hang on a bit longer. I did so until it was possible to get a boat round and we were able to bundle the man in".

HMS Snaefell (previously Cambell's PS Waverley) was lost in a bombing raid off Sunderland on July 5th 1941, so by the end of the year the 8th was down to 6 ships: Glen Avon, Glen Usk, Glenmore, Laguna Belle, Medway Queen and Thames Queen, all at North Shields. The wreck of HMS Snaefell was discovered by the "Silent Running" dive team 8 miles off Sunderland in 2010. The forward part of the ship had been shattered by the bomb hit and many empty cartridge cases were found suggesting a fierce fight.

The naval movement log for HMS Medway Queen shows her at "Tyne" for most of 1941 and 1942. Movements were made elsewhere such as to Stornoway, Methil, Harwich, Leith and Rosyth but only for short periods. She was taken in hand at Leith for a refit on 21st September 1942 until 20th October.

Gradually more purpose built minesweepers became available. Augmenting the Halcyon class, 22 ships were bought in 1941 under the lend-lease agreement and over 700 purpose designed ships were built during the war. By 1943 there was less dependence on the surviving paddle minesweepers which could be better used elsewhere. Paddlesteamers had disadvantages as

GUN CREW IN TRAINING.

ROBBIE ?

JIM DAY

ARTHUR MARAGA

ALBERT NASON

CHARLIE WALKER

BRUCE SUTTON

JIMMY JAMES

"SPOT"

Photographs above and opposite - Eric Woodroffe, and MQPS Collection.

minesweepers. They had a limited radius of action, the paddles were vulnerable and it was officially considered "difficult to keep them afloat after hitting a mine".

Some were converted for other roles and some were assigned to training units. Medway Queen was in Great Yarmouth on 29th January 1943 when the movement record is marked as "discontinued". It is likely that it was on this date that she was re-assigned to the training programme and then moved to Scotland.

Minesweeper training was centred on HMS Lochinvar; a shore establishment set up in 1939 at Port Edgar on the Firth of Forth. In 1943 it was temporarily moved to Granton Harbour, Edinburgh (until 1946) while the former site was used for Normandy landings preparations.

Minesweeping officer trainees were carefully selected with particular regard to their technical and navigational abilities. Their six week course at HMS Lochinvar started with a couple of days practical work on board one of the training vessels, then an intensive on-shore programme of instruction, followed by a 3 week period of hands on training on ships with additional accommodation for them.

One such trainee, Sub Lieutenant Ron Lattimore RNVR seconded to Medway Queen while awaiting his posting, remembered many years afterwards that on completion of the day's practice sweeping the ship turned for home and the sweeping gear was replaced by a trawl net. A practice no doubt inspired by the continued presence of ex-fishermen in the minesweeping flotillas. The catch would be sold to local restaurants and "chippies" on return to base.

Charles McAra joined Medway Queen as First Lieutenant early in 1945. At that time she had a ship's company of 4 officers and 24 ratings and there was accommodation for up to 20 trainees. Her behaviour was rather different to that of a screw powered ship. The lack of propeller thrust against the rudder makes for a wide turning circle, even in the best conditions, and McAra notes that "Medway Queen answered the helm in her own time". On the other hand she could stop very smartly indeed. "Stop Engines" had an immediate effect on her speed and a kick astern stopped her immediately. Paddle steamers tend to roll and in heavy weather a paddle can lift clear of the water making progress erratic. This was countered by rolling 5cwt (254kg) mine sinkers from one side of the deck to the other to restore her trim.

Medway Queen had established a reputation for treating the trainees sent to her as guests and the ship's cook was crucial to maintaining this standard. The wardroom had retained the qualities of an excursion steamer saloon and seemed more like a restaurant than part of a warship. A roaring coal fire, pre lunch drinks and then roast beef followed by a pudding with custard made a marked contrast to the conditions on an exposed deck in the North Sea.

The routine was as regular as clockwork. At 9am she would leave harbour, towed out stern first by a tug, and proceed eastwards down the Firth of Forth to practice the use of the Oropesa gear to sweep mines. The need for mine clearance lasted beyond the end of hostilities so training continued. During the war the Royal Navy alone had laid over 186,000 mines in defensive fields and 77,000 in offensive operations. Mines had been used in great quantities by all combatants and all would have to be cleared the hard way.

The war in Europe came to an end in May 1945. On VE Day, Tuesday 8th May, the flotilla remained in harbour and there was a service of thanksgiving on the West Pier in the morning. At 3pm all the ships in harbour sounded their sirens and rang their bells – for about half an hour. Changes began to take place as men were "demobbed" back into civilian life, ships were decommissioned and bases closed. All three armed services still had a tough job to do but the reductions began almost immediately. Medway Queen's complement began to change. Lieutenant McAra was appointed captain and had Lieutenant J. James RNVR as First Lieutenant.

When Medway Queen's own time came to leave the Royal Navy she was to be sent to Thorneycroft's ship yard in Southampton to be refitted. Despite having spent years at sea during the war a survey was ordered and it was decided that she was unstable. The surveyor signalled the Admiralty and CinC Rosyth as follows *"MOST IMMEDIATE MEDWAY QUEEN TO REMAIN IN HARBOUR AND IN NO CIRCUMSTANCES TO BE SAILED ANYWHERE UNTIL MODIFICATIONS HAVE BEEN CARRIED OUT STOP DETAILS OF THESE WILL FOLLOW"*

All unnecessary top weight including the armament and minesweeping equipment was removed, the storm doors on the companionway strengthened and a breakwater fitted aft to prevent damage by a following sea. Lt. James was in command for the journey South. which was to be undertaken in daylight and in the event of bad weather they were ordered to take shelter in the nearest harbour; a marked change from the attitudes of the previous years.

4
DUNKIRK

I have always found two particular operations from WWII especially interesting. One is the D-Day landings because of the years of meticulous planning that went into it and the logistical detail required. The other is operation "Dynamo", the evacuation from Dunkirk; for the opposite reason that the incredible logistics were not pre-planned but managed on a minute by minute basis as the event unfolded. It is not possible to do justice to Dunkirk in one short chapter but here is Medway Queen's part in the evacuation set in context of the wider events taking place and with an overview of the other NMSPCo ships taking part.

The "phoney war" on land ended with the Norwegian campaign and on 10th May 1940 the German Army launched its attack on France, through Holland and Belgium. On the 13th a second attack entered France at Sedan. After breaking through, German armour headed for the Channel to trap the allied armies. Outgunned and out-manoevered, the allies fell back towards the coast and, with the loss of Boulogne on 25th May and Calais on the 26th, were forced into an ever smaller perimeter. Destroyers evacuating the army from Boulogne duelled at close range with the panzers as they entered the

harbour area - the tanks lost in that encounter. The British Expeditionary Force and the French First Army retreated towards Dunkirk (Dunquerque). Dunkirk had much to recommend it with a large modern port and miles of gently sloping beaches. In the event, however, most of the port was unusable and the majority of the men had to be loaded via the East Mole or the beaches themselves.

The only way out for the British soldiers was evacuation by sea. The Royal Navy had realised this and had been planning for the eventuality. Vice Admiral Bertram Ramsay was put in charge and had less than a week of preparation before the official order to begin operation Dynamo was issued at 1857 on Sunday 26th May. Before that, however, a number of troops had been evacuated by destroyers and other ships and the despatch of personnel vessels (mainly cross channel ferries) had started at 1500 on the 26th with the intention of providing 2 ships every 4 hours. The first of these returned at 2230 and landed 1,312 men. Preparations for the full scale evacuation intensified. Orders were given and stores issued. Hundreds of ships and boats were allocated to the task.

HMS Medway Queen, Ramsgate 1940. PSPS Collection

HMS Gracie Fields. Eric Woodroffe.

A group of ships from the 7th and 10th minesweeping flotillas were at anchor near Dover. On that Sunday extra stores were issued and the officers and wireless operators were called to briefing sessions. According to the cook's assistant, "Sec", there was enough "to feed a ruddy army". Thomas Russell, the cook, wrote an account of the operation and referred only to "Sec". We now understand that "Sec's" name was Mr. Stanley Bell. Medway Queen's commanding officer, Lieutenant A. T. Cook RNR, gave orders at about 1700 to start preparations to feed several hundred "somewhat peckish" men, who were expected on board later. using the newly arrived stores. At 1900 the flotilla weighed anchor and the eight paddlers steamed in line ahead towards Dunkirk.

On that first trip the gunfire was mostly inland away from the beaches and the troops being picked up were mostly base staff rather than combat soldiers. The threat of air attack was reduced by the presence of an Anti-aircraft cruiser, HMS Calcutta, but the situation was chaotic. The ships anchored offshore and used their own boats to collect men from the beaches. A hard night ensued with the boats shuttling back and forth. The soldiers, waiting in long lines on the beach and down into the surf, mostly had little experience of boats and were inclined to swamp them when too many tried to board at once. Threats and occasional force were used to control that situation but even so plenty of baling was required just to remove the water draining from the soldier's uniforms. AB Albert Skinner who was in charge of one of Medway Queen's boats recalled afterwards that "not one of the soldiers had let go their rifles except in the case of a blinded man and then his rifle was carried by one of the men".

Once on board the soldiers had to be fed. Cook Thomas Russell and his assistant had spent the voyage over preparing huge quantities of sandwiches, Irish stew and

Brighton Belle in peacetime.
Stanley Abrahams

Taken from Medway Queen, HMS Brighton Belle is seen sinking with a tug alongside. Eric Woodroffe.

"Navy Cocoa". Thomas Russell described the scene: *"These weren't peckish men they were starving animals, most of them too desperately hungry to be polite – pushing, shoving and shouting. Someone opened the starboard half door and they started to flood for service right into the galley, then they tried to exit through the other door. Sec and I were serving as fast as we could but we were getting shoved back and forth and could scarcely manage. Some of the lads started to help themselves, it was pandemonium."* Mr. Russell pushed his way out and found a ship's officer who restored order. The Irish stew ran out about halfway back and by the time they entered harbour the two men had served huge quantities of food and drink to their passengers.

The journey back was not without incident. The flotilla left the beaches at about 0700 on the 28th of May and proceeded to Dover. Just outside the harbour an air raid developed during which Medway Queen's gunners shot down an enemy fighter aircraft. HMS Brighton Belle collided with a submerged wreck and began to sink. A tug stood by as Medway Queen went alongside and took off all the soldiers and crew before the ship sank. The captain and even the ship's dog were saved. Seriously overloaded, they then completed the journey to Dover and landed the troops. Before they could rest the ship had to be cleaned, ready for the next trip. Mud and sand were everywhere, plus abandoned kit, rifles, cigarette packets, bottles and paper and worst of all the results of sea-sickness. The whole ship had to be washed down. The galley crew still had to prepare meals for the ship's company and snatch what rest they could between times.

The flotilla left Dover for their second trip at 1700 on the 28th and steamed for Dunkirk, this time headed for the harbour. HMS Gracie Fields was bombed and sunk on the way. The sea was unusually phosphorescent and Medway Queen's wake acted as a bright marker to the German bombers. Oil bags were lowered into the sea to reduce this effect. Then, creeping past Gravelines on the French coast sparks from a soot fire in the funnel gave their position away to the shore batteries. A bucket chain was formed and water used to douse the fire – an action that proved unpopular with the engine room crew!

They were shelled as they entered the harbour and the burning oil tanks cast a dark pall of smoke everywhere whilst also lighting the scene. The harbour was already wrecked at this stage. Buildings and docks reduced to rubble and sunken ships everywhere. Most of it was unusable but a long concrete jetty, the East Mole, remained intact and it was possible to berth ships along both sides. A similar structure on the West side was used by the French Navy. As the operation went on ships became sunk alongside it and damage from bombs and shells was repaired as best they could with planks, mess tables or anything that could be found. This became the exit route for around two thirds of the soldiers rescued from Dunkirk. Medway Queen went alongside. Scaling ladders had to be used as Medway Queen's decks were below the level of the mole but loading was considerably faster than using boats from the beaches. The ships of the

Dunkirk Evacuation. PSPS Collection

flotilla were now acting independently and as soon as a ship was full it left for home, making way for another. Medway Queen headed back to Britain, this time to Ramsgate which was to be her base for the remainder of Operation Dynamo.

The early stages of the evacuation were undoubtedly chaotic. However, as the operation proceeded the naval beach parties under the command of Captain W.G. Tennant RN took control and although mistakes and some confusion were always there the situation improved. Rear Admiral W.F Wake-Walker was Flag Officer Afloat and Commander J.C. Clouston was in charge of embarkation on the Mole. He was killed while returning to Dunkirk for the last pickup on June 3rd. Commanders H. Richardson and T. Kerr were in charge at Bray Dunes. There were serious problems loading men from the beaches. The ships did not have enough boats and loading in the surf was slow and dangerous. The first of these problems was solved by the legendary "little ships". Hundreds of small craft were requisitioned and, from May 29th, were taken to Dunkirk to ferry men to the

ships from the beaches. Most had naval crews but many were manned by civilians, often their owners. Some were there completely "unofficially". When they returned to England these little ships invariably brought back more men than was safe for them to carry. The second problem, loading in the surf, was partly alleviated by the creation of lorry jetties. Several of these sprang up along the coast where lines of abandoned lorries were pushed into the sea and lashed together. With their tyres shot out and an improvised walkway of planks etc on top they formed a usable pier. They were not stable enough for ships or even large boats but the small craft could load from them quickly and safely. The evacuation proceeded day and night at first but as the enemy closed in and air attacks intensified the emphasis changed to predominantly night time operations.

A number of other GSN and New Medway ships were involved in the evacuation. HMS Queen of Thanet had sailed in the same group as Medway Queen at the start and over the course of the operation made 4 return trips and brought home 4000 men. Queen of the Channel was

Dunkirk evacuees on board Medway Queen.
PSPS Collection

Dunkirk East Mole and Harbour and hospital ship.
PSPS Collection

lost on 28th May. She had arrived at the mole and loaded over 900 troops but was bombed and sunk on her return journey. HMS Crested Eagle was also bombed and sunk on 29th. Royal Daffodil was a much larger and faster ship than Medway Queen. She too made seven trips to Dunkirk and before being seriously damaged on 2nd of June. Royal Sovereign, HMS Royal Eagle and HMS Golden Eagle were also there.

Medway Queen settled into the routine; the men who were there and have written about it make the whole thing sound like a regular ferry service. Each night would be filled with the noise and danger of battle. Sometimes they were directed to the Mole and at others to the beaches, according to circumstances. Each day was taken up with repairs, cleaning and restocking supplies, ammunition and fuel. The ship's First Lieutenant, Sub Lieutenant J.D. Graves RNR wrote a very detailed account after the war and recorded many incidents. On the third trip the ship acquired a sandbagged enclosure on

Lt Cdr, A. T. Cook RNR, who as a Lieutenant captained Medway Queen at Dunkirk - courtesy Mrs P. Kennedy.

naval officer finding the ship had gone signalled Dover and at some stage the signal was misinterpreted and Medway Queen was reported as lost. This was broadcast on the midnight news and the crew's families had an anxious wait until the error was corrected on the 7am news.

Another narrow escape happened when Medway Queen was directed by a naval officer in a motor boat to a point up the coast where a number of troops were said to be cut off. By chance they had some Spaniards aboard who had escaped from there and who said that it had been in enemy hands for two days. Another ship was less fortunate, fell into the trap and was sunk. A destroyer, now aware of what was happening opened fire when hailed and sank the motor boat. Graves says this is when they were posted missing because they were so late so it is quite likely, therefore, that the two incidents occurred on the same trip and both contributed to the confusion.

Chief Engineer Davis was in charge of the Medway Queen's engines and kept them running throughout the operation, never leaving his post while the ship was at sea. Some of the men rescued were later to repay their debt by supporting the preservation society and still remember their rescue with great emotion. John Howarth from Rochester was in the middle of the Channel surrounded by bodies and almost resigned to death when, over the horizon, came the Medway Queen on her way back to England crammed with troops. He could hardly believe his luck when the ship paused to pick him up!

the afterdeck with 2 Bren guns manned by RASC cadets who had volunteered. Medway Queen supplemented this firepower with more Bren guns picked up from the beaches, lashed in position wherever possible and provided with ammunition. There was no shortage of soldiers willing to fire them. Other soldiers were encouraged to fire at aircraft with their rifles. The total result was a storm of lead which aided the ship's survival and led to three low flying aircraft claimed shot down by Medway Queen during the operation.

On another trip, perhaps the fourth, Medway Queen was loading at the mole when the naval officer in charge suspended loading to concentrate on a larger vessel lying astern. Albert Skinner describes how a destroyer cut their stern mooring rope and the ship drifted out. The Captain ordered the head rope to be cut also and after striking another ship a glancing blow Medway Queen found she could not get back to the mole and headed away with what she had. In the confusion the senior

A French soldier, Paul Dervilers remembered his rescue; "*I was on the beach walking up the coast towards Belgium when I saw some Englishmen getting into a dinghy and I joined ten of them who tried to get aboard. But the dinghy became waterlogged. We all began bailing hopelessly with our helmets. Fortunately, half-way to an off-lying ship, we picked up an abandoned little skiff in good shape and we got into it. It was 2300 when we climbed up the ladder of the Medway Queen.*"

The British evacuation was officially completed at 2230 on Sunday 2nd of June when the SNO Dunkirk signalled "BEF Evacuated". Ships waiting for the French rearguard left empty because they did not arrive as scheduled. There had been a delay in making a planned counter attack which did not take place until the evening. A further trip was called for on the night of 3-4th June to take off the French. Vice Admiral Ramsay had made it clear to the Admiralty that this was the last effort. If the evacuation was to continue beyond this night then fresh crews would have to be found.

The French rearguard was picked up from the East Mole,

starting at 2230 on 3rd of June. Ships including Medway Queen were assigned to the task and worked as quickly as possible to move the men. While loading, a ship astern of Medway Queen was hit (or possibly suffered a near miss) by a shell or bomb and driven into the paddle box causing some damage. Medway Queen's final act in the evacuation is described by Lieutenant Graves: *"About 1am our captain nursed us clear of the berth, with difficulty because of the damaged sponson. And Medway Queen made off very slowly down the harbour under the sure hands of Lieutenant Jolly with the familiar Mole still lit by blazing oil tanks falling astern and Lieutenant Keilly strumming a mandolin on the after deck."* On their return Admiral Ramsay signalled his appreciation with "Well done Medway Queen".

The last ships to leave the Mole were the destroyers Express (at 0318) and Shikari (0340). 27000 troops had been picked up that night and "Dynamo" was terminated by the Admiralty. Reconnaissance sweeps of the channel continued, to look for survivors in small boats.

Landing the men at Dover, Ramsgate and the other ports was not the end of their story. In an incredible feat of organisation the Southern Railway Company moved hundreds of thousands of men away from their arrival points to inland reception areas. At its peak, on the 1st of June, over 63000 men were moved in one day. Trains of 10 carriages each were loaned by all the main line railway companies. The Southern Railway provided locomotives and crews for at least the first part of the journey and the 10 carriages standard meant that they had a wide range of locomotives able to move any of the trains. Trains were held in sidings, or queued on the Hothfield to Ashford West branch line, and moved into the ports as needed. For example, in Dover there was always one train loading and one waiting. When a full train left they loaded the other one and a replacement "waiting" train moved in. Despatch and en-route control was all by telephone.

Frequently, the destination and final route was not decided until after the train was on its way. Feeding points were set up at nominated stations where officials and volunteers provided tea, sandwiches, cigarettes, etc. to the men. There was often a real problem getting the tea mugs back as the train moved off! Ambulance trains for the severely wounded were also provided when required.

The army had lost most of its heavy equipment but Dunkirk had saved hundreds of thousands of trained soldiers who now had a good idea of what they were up against. With the Commonwealth divisions and other units already in the country they would be quite capable of undertaking their traditional role as "Goal Keeper for

Sub Lieutenant John Graves.   PSPS Collection

the Navy" had an invasion been attempted.

There are endless facts and figures relating to Dunkirk. Reports and statistics often conflict and Admiral Ramsay in his official report states clearly that the official total of men landed is an underestimate. Under these circumstances the Medway Queen's crew's estimate of 7000 men rescued and 3 aircraft destroyed are as good a summary as any. In Admiral Ramsay's own words:

"WELL DONE MEDWAY QUEEN"

As a result of their endeavours throughout the evacuation, a number of Medway Queen's crew received awards. The DSC was awarded to Lieutenant A.T. Cook RNR and to Sub-lieutenant J. D. Graves RNR. The DSM was awarded to Petty Officers A. E. Crossley RFR and H. J. McAllister RFR and to Seaman K. R. Olly RNR. Second Engineer T. Irwin and Fireman J. D. Connell were both mentioned in despatches.

Medway Queen leaving Herne Bay.
Kent History & Library centre, Maidstone.

5
POST-WAR SERVICE

The first New Medway ship back in service after the war was Queen of Thanet. She had been released by the War Department in 1945 and was reconditioned at the company's own yard in Rochester. Her first trip was on VE Day, 8th June 1946. The service ran to Margate and Southend with cruises in areas deemed safe from wartime minefields and wreckage. A surviving leaflet from September 1946 gives a sailing time of 3pm from Southend Pier for one of these cruises; "A VOYAGE OF SPECIAL INTEREST". The itinerary included viewing war time shipwrecks, boom defenses and the anti-aircraft forts in the Thames. Eight wrecks are listed: SS. Pinewood, Castor, Richard Montgomery, Belvedere, Inver, Araby, Beneficent and Arinia. Adult fare was 3 shillings and the ship returned at 4.45pm

Queen of Kent was released in 1946 and although in poor condition was reconditioned for use as a stop-gap until the modern replacement ships became available. For the 1947 season all three surviving paddlers were available. Queen of Kent and Queen of Thanet were operated until 1949. The GSN and New Medway fleets were jointly marketed as "Eagle and Queen Line steamers". They retained their own fleet identities but effectively were one company.

Medway Queen was very thoroughly refitted in Southampton by J. I. Thorneycroft of Woolston, and surviving correspondence from the New Medway company underlines just how anxious they were to have her back for the 1947 season. The hull was stripped, chipped and cleaned back to bare metal and then rebuilt to closely resemble her pre-war appearance. The rebuild resulted in extra weight which increased her draught by 1½ inches (38mm). Before the war, she had been permitted to carry 980 passengers at a speed of 15 knots but this was now reduced to a maximum of 828 plus a crew of 30 and she was allowed a top speed of 13 knots. During this refit, or shortly afterwards, crests bearing the "Invicta" motif were attached to either side of the ship's funnel.

The season started on 24th May 1947 but did not get off to a completely clean start for the company as PS Queen of Thanet damaged a paddlewheel in collision with the pier and had to be towed back to the yard in Rochester. Medway Queen and her crew under Captain Leonard Horsham soon settled into their regular routine. Herne Bay does not feature on the 1947 timetable, although the pier was open for business in that year, but by 1950 it was included in Medway Queen's itinerary.

In 1949 the Herne Bay trips were undertaken by MV Rochester Queen. Medway Queen's route was Rochester, Chatham, Sheerness and Southend with two sailings daily except Fridays. The ship usually did not operate on Fridays, quite why is unclear – perhaps it was treated as a preparation day. There would have been few day trippers on that day and most holiday makers would be going home on the following day. The regular service was supplemented with occasional excursions elsewhere. In that first post-war season a day return from Chatham to Southend-on-Sea cost 5/6d Equivalent to £23.20 today based on average earnings differences.

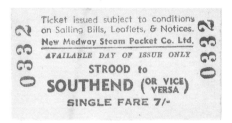

MV Royal Daffodil, had continued as a troop ship immediately after the war and was then refitted in 1947 and used on the cross-channel services. Replacements for the other two motor vessels which had been sunk were not yet available. The new MV Royal Sovereign was launched in 1948 and MV Queen of the Channel in 1949. Both were built by William Denny & Bros Ltd. of Dumbarton. Their arrival allowed the sale of the two older paddlers to the Red Funnel Steamers of Southampton. Queen of Thanet was renamed Solent Queen. She was sold for scrap in 1951 after catching fire whilst in dry dock. Queen of Kent was renamed Lorna Doone and operated until 1952 when she too was scrapped.

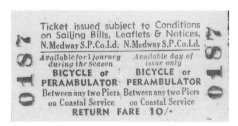

In the seasons of 1952 and '53 Dawn Fenwick (now Mrs. Dawn Mattocks) and her friend Barbara, the daughter of Mr.Tom Gibbs the Chief Steward, worked on board Medway Queen. She thought herself lucky to land such a very privileged and exciting job! The alternatives would have been much more mundane.

Dining Saloon c1955. PSPS Collection.

"The fact that Barbara's father was the Chief Steward did not do us any favours as we were expected to pull our weight and work hard, which we did! It was obvious to me from my very first day that this was a very happy ship. My area of work was to be the upper aft saloon with the windows dressed in deep red velvet curtains, in those days a suggestion of luxury and style! Mrs.Osborn was the Catering Manageress and her responsibilities included the bars and ice cream kiosk. In my days, we served mainly sandwiches and snacks plus the usual beverages. I also had to help out in the ice cream kiosk as and when required. The saloon had to be kept clean at all times, Clearing the tables after passengers had vacated was a number one requirement, leaving a "sticky" table was a cardinal sin. Limited hot meals were prepared in the galley and served in the saloon. Meat was still on ration, until July 1954, but the traditional "Plaice & Chips" was available for those passengers that could afford it. They were austere days and money was in short supply for the average family so a day on a Medway steamer was a big day out!

The lower saloons were the bars and from time to time I was called upon to pop down and clear glasses and tidy up. Keeping the ship "Ship shape and Bristol fashion" was not just a saying on Medway Queen, it was a total requirement. The Captain kept a close eye on things at all times; no comment was made in front of the passengers but at the end of the day those responsible for anything that was not up to scratch were called before him and given a severe telling off! However, this was not a regular occurrence as the crew worked for each other and in general the ship was kept "spick & span"! The ship was their pride as well!

What was great to see were the passengers embarking at the piers. There was always a large contingent at Sun Pier, Chatham, and to see their happy faces of delight and expectation of a great day out was excitement in itself. After the war years and the austerity that followed this was a really big treat for them all. There was no casual wear in those days, it was either working gear or Sunday best and a trip on the Medway Queen warranted the latter! After dropping and picking up passengers at Southend it was on to Herne Bay. Short sea cruises were arranged to produce more revenue before the final trip back to Medway in the cool and sometimes chilly air where tired passengers relaxed sitting on the warm funnel box, no doubt reflecting on a great day out on the Medway Queen."

George Painter also remembers a non-landing evening cruise to Southend and back in 1952 He was accompanied by his future wife Iris and remembers a "plaice and chips" supper in the forward saloon and later Iris feeling a little "woozy" but not sea sick. There was always a bit of a sway on the Medway Queen, even in calm waters, sometimes, the captain requesting passengers to move to either side of the ship to maintain a balance!

A major variation in the routine came in 1953 when Medway Queen attended the Coronation Review at Spithead, not just as an excursion steamer but as part of the official line up. This "day in the limelight" is covered in a chapter of its own later in the book. After the event, Medway Queen made an overnight dash back to the Medway to be ready for her regular passengers.

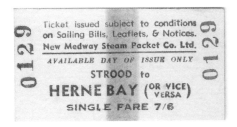

In order to comply with regulations regarding navigation lights, Medway Queen was fitted with a high bracket on her funnel in 1954 for navigation lights. This is also a great help in dating photographs; pre-war will not show the funnel crests and the presence of the bracket indicates 1954 or later.

The schedule changed slightly with the closure of Sheerness Pier in 1955 and from the 1957 season Clacton was added to the itinerary on some days including cruises from there to the river Blackwater.

MQPS member Len Knight remembers an unfortunate incident resulting in the death of a crew member. It happened in the summer of 1958 when the ship had just left Sun Pier on her way to Southend. It was quite common for crew members to come out on the paddle sponsons and get water to wash them down. The method was to fill a bucket by lowering it into the sea on a rope and then pulling it out full. In this case a young and inexperienced seaman, Colin Sellars, did not allow for the drag of the bucket and was pulled off balance and into the water. He grabbed another crew member, Mr. Crispe, to try and regain his balance but pulled him in as well.

By the time the passengers realised what had happened they were out of reach of a thrown lifebelt. Len shouted "Man overboard" and ran to the bridge. It took a while to explain the situation. Meanwhile a boat had put out from the nearby Chatham Dockyard. They pulled Mr. Crispe from the water but were unable to find the younger man. Once convinced of the seriousness of the situation the captain reversed Medway Queen back to the boat. Mr

Crispe was taken back on board and the ship returned to Sun Pier. The police were called, statements made and the journey eventually continued in a very subdued mood. The young man's body was not recovered for some days.

There were of course very many happier days on board. Medway Queen is fondly remembered, not only in the areas where she operated but by people who holidayed or visited there as well She made appearances in a number of feature films and radio/TV programmes including *Dunkirk* (Ealing Films 1958) and Kenneth Russell's first-ever film, *French Dressing* (1964). Sadly, "Dunkirk"'s budget did not include returning the ship to her wartime appearance and she was shown in her civilian guise.

A comparison of fares over the years is interesting. Taking adult day return fares between Southend and Herne Bay with 2012 equivalents based on average earnings we get:

1950 6/6d	(£25.20)
1953 7/-	(£20.60)
1960 8/6d	(£18.30)
1963 10/-	(£18.00)

MQPS member Mr. Bob Harragan remembers Medway Queen in the late 1950s from a holiday in Herne Bay: *"You could set your clock by the Medway Queen. First a plume of smoke would appear over the sea, then the hull would appear in view from the holiday chalets on the outskirts of Herne Bay and she would pass, paddle-wheels thrashing, as she headed just round the corner to the town pier. But it was me who talked them into an excursion on the Queen. I was probably four years old and very brave but nervous on that day in the late 1950s. The Queen seemed enormous to me, but not so big you didn't have to descend to a platform nearer the water to embark at the end of the pier.*

That platform, I recall, was an ironwork grill, with seemingly giant brownish waves washing about underneath. I clung to my mother's skirts. On board I huddled on a seat close to the superstructure, flattening myself against it, as far from the sea as possible. At my feet was a plastic yellow bucket, the sort you build sandcastles with, and it began to roll in circles across the deck. I wailed, but wouldn't move. My Dad just took a step and picked it up. Then he took me away from the great expanse of water, down to the engine room. It was probably less through my discomfort on deck than his fascination with engineering. He and my uncle had even built their first car. But I loved it below, too. My memories are of a catwalk running the length of the seemingly enormous engine. Much was painted a deep green."

The Family Album

In 1960 Medway Queen was alternately sailing from Southend to Herne Bay or Clacton. The day would have started at Strood with a sailing to Southend on Sea via Chatham and would have ended with the return trip. Passengers from Herne Bay went to Southend with a decent time ashore, followed by a cruise to Strood where they changed to rail travel back to their start. According to handbills in my collection, in 1961 this cost 12/6d (£26.10 in 2012 wages).and by 1963 it had risen to 14/- (£25.20 in 2012 wages). Southend, whose pier was reckoned to be one of the longest anywhere, was equipped with a tram to whisk passengers from the pier head to the promenade.

As maintenance costs increased paddle steamers were withdrawn all around the country. In some cases they were replaced by more modern vessels with lower maintenance costs and in others the routes were completely closed down as holiday makers found other ways of spending their time and money. Medway Queen had been the last paddler on the Thames and Medway since 1949 and by the end of the 1963 season impending maintenance requirements made continued operation uneconomic. Her last voyage to Southend was on 9th September 1963 at the close of the season. Even at that time the ship was considered to be of sufficient interest that the national press covered the event. On the last leg of the voyage, returning from Southend to Strood she was given a massive send off from Southend pier. The RNLI lifeboat escorted her, streamers were thrown and music and a mayoral address were played over the pier's PA system. On arrival at the entrance to the river Medway a greeting was flashed from the Port Operations HQ on Garrison Point. She received a gun salute and the Medway Conservancy Council's launch, Medway Leader, escorted her into the river's mouth. The ship made her way slowly up river to Strood where a small crowd had gathered to watch her last arrival. Captain Leonard Horsham rang down "Stop Engines" for the last time.

This page and opposite - *A trip on the Medway Queen was the highlight of many family holidays and warranted a picture for the family album. Thanks to Charles Hewett, Alan Wright, Gail Coleshill, Carol Fishpool, David Morris, Mr. H. Anderson. and the "War and Peace Collection" for their contributions to these pages.*

As early as 1961 Mr. W. G. Prynne of the Paddle Steamer Preservation Society (PSPS) had contacted the GSN Chairman, a Mr. Grout, on the subject of Medway Queen's future. He suggested that when the ship was eventually withdrawn from service she should be preserved as the last of the Thames steamers and in recognition of her part in the Dunkirk story. GSN's response was encouraging and a PSPS sub committee was formed so as to be prepared when the time came. In the summer of 1963, when action became necessary, the GSN board responded sympathetically; granting the society time for planning and fund-raising. They also made clear, though, that they could not afford to keep the ship in service and that they would not permit a solution that saw her in competition with their own operation. Little did Bill Prynne realise just how long the fight to save her would go on for!

A public meeting was called in the Baltic Exchange for the 18th October with the backing of GSN and the PSPS central committee. Enthusiastic press support for the campaign resulted in around 100 people attending. It was decided to launch an appeal and to create the Medway Queen Trust to oversee the campaign. Representatives of the Dunkirk Veteran's Association joined the committee which met under the chairmanship of Professor Alan Robinson who was also President of the PSPS.

Money flowed in through the appeal but although the subscription list ran into hundreds of people it was unable to reach the £7000 target that was considered necessary

Margate c1960. PSPS Collection.

Approaching Southend, 31 August 1963. PSPS Collection.

Medway Queen arriving at Southend. Richard Danielson Collection.

Medway Queen leaving Southend, 31 August 1963. PSPS Collection.

From 2nd JUNE until 8th SEPT. 1963
Every SUNDAY, TUESDAY and THURSDAY

THE POPULAR PADDLE STEAMER
'MEDWAY QUEEN'

will sail from SOUTHEND PIER

at 11.0 a.m.

to HERNE BAY

ALLOWING UP TO 4½ HOURS ASHORE

FARES
SINGLE 7/-   DAY RETURN 11/-   PERIOD RETURN 13/-

This excursion offers up to 3 hours in the
ANCIENT CITY OF CANTERBURY
DAY RETURN (BOAT/BUS) 14/-   CHILD 3-14 yrs. 7/3

OUT   TIMES   HOME
Depart Southend 11.00 a.m.   Depart Herne Bay 5.00 p.m.
Due Herne Bay 12.30 p.m.   Due Southend : 6.40 p.m.

Passengers must leave CANTERBURY by 3.55 p.m. to connect with Steamer at Herne Bay

NON-LANDING   Depart Southend 11.0 a.m. back at 2.15 p.m.   FARE
TRIPS to HERNE BAY   Depart Southend 3.15 p.m. back at 6.40 p.m.   7/6

Children: under 14 yrs. half above fares (except where otherwise shown) under 3 yrs. free
Tickets Booked at the Pier Hill Office (Shore End) Include Admission to the Pier

Catering, Refreshments and Fully Licensed Bars on Board

Sailings subject to weather and other circumstances permitting
SPECIAL RATES FOR PARTIES BOOKED IN ADVANCE

EAGLE & QUEEN LINE STEAMERS
PIER HILL, SOUTHEND-ON-SEA   PHONE: 66597 (MAY/SEPT)
FOR CONDITIONS OF CARRIAGE SEE OVERLEAF

Dunkirk 25th anniversary commemorations. A survey of the ship was arranged and Medway Queen was towed up river to Rotherhithe with the assistance of PSPS volunteers. One of the survey team was John Graves who had been the ship's First Lieutenant at Dunkirk but the survey showed that the cost of making her fully seaworthy would be exorbitant. Hardly surprising since that was one of the reasons for her withdrawal. The National Trust persevered however, looking for uses to which the ship could be put and seeking a long term static role to follow.

By July 1964 these avenues had been exhausted without success but the National Trust had managed to interest catering company Fortes in the ship. One of the factors behind Fortes' interest was the publicity value of a well known ship which was getting lots of very positive press coverage. In another last-minute action Fortes purchased the ship and battled for almost a year to get the necessary licences to operate Medway Queen as a restaurant on the Thames Embankment. Despite support from the press, London County Council and Westminster City Council a group of residents, fearing the effect on their property values, ensured that the necessary licenses were not granted and the plan foundered.

Fortes had no choice but to sell the ship to the highest bidder and that meant a breaker. The Medway Queen Trust swung into action, once more relying on the national press, especially the Daily Mail, to energise public opinion. Never-the-less a sale was arranged to a Belgian ship breaker and Medway Queen was prepared for the cross channel journey. In the event, Mr. Pierre Van Heyghen head of the Belgian ship breaking company was very sympathetic to the public mood and to the history of the vessel and when yet another last minute saviour turned up he willingly cooperated. The Daily Mail, on Saturday 21st August 1965, reported Mr. Van Heyghen as saying "If I had been told of this a week ago I would have withdrawn my offer and the men who have fought to save her might have got her at a cheaper price."

to purchase the ship. This amount would be £252000 in today's money, calculated by average earnings but there was no Heritage Lottery Fund available then. GSN had given the trust until the end of 1963 and at the last minute the National Trust took an interest. They thought she could be used in support of "Enterprise Neptune" (an appeal to preserve sections of coastline) by steaming around Britain and being used to host receptions in aid of the appeal. Afterwards she could also take part in the

Medway Queen early 1950s. R Wright

Medway Queen at Sun Pier. War & Peace Collection.

Signed drawing - Duncan Harper, then aged 14.

Opposite top left - *Captain Horsham c1963. PSPS Collection.*
Opposite top right *- Dining Saloon c1955. PSPS Collection.*
Opposite bottom *- Promenade Deck, 31 August 1963. PSPS Collection.*
Above - *Medway Queen at Sun Pier. War and Peace Collection.*

Right - *Rotherhythe, January 1964. PSPS Collection.*

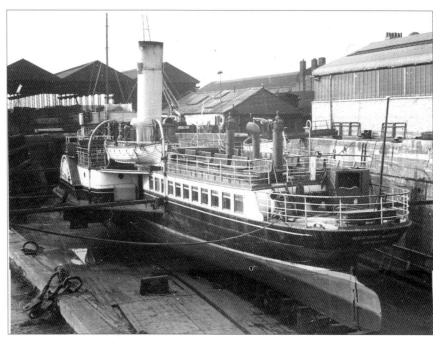

Above - Approaching Southend. Rodger Stockman.

Below - Medway Queen from Sun Pier 1963.

Ticket issued subject to Conditions
on Sailing Bills, Leaflets, & Notices.
N.Medway S.P.Co.Ld. N.Medway S.P.Co.Ld.

1432

Available day of issue only | Available day of issue only

Herne Bay to **STROOD** | **STROOD** to **HERNE BAY**
FARE 11/- | FARE 11/-

1432

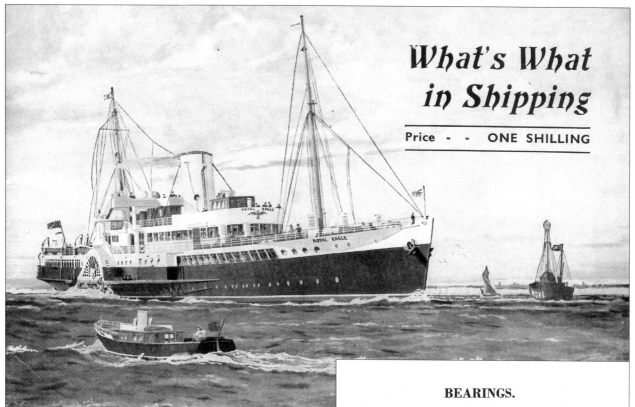

What's What in Shipping

Price - - ONE SHILLING

BEARINGS.

When objects are sighted their bearing (direction) is reported to the bridge as follows :—

" Right ahead (lighthouse)."

" On starboard bow (sloop.)"

" On starboard beam (buoy)."

" On starboard quarter (speed-boat)."

" Astern (life buoy)."

PIER-TO-PIER DISTANCES.

Teddington to Tower Pier	...	...	18	nautical miles.
Tower Pier to Greenwich	...	...	4·25	,,	,,
Greenwich to North Woolwich	...	4	,,	,,
North Woolwich to Tilbury	...	...	14·55	,,	,,
Tilbury to Southend	...	...	16	,,	,,
Southend to Clacton	...	...	35·5	,,	,,
Southend to Sheerness	...	...	6	,,	,,
Southend to Chatham	...	...	17	,,	,,
Southend to Herne Bay	...	...	18	,,	,,
Southend to Margate	...	...	28	,,	,,
Southend to Ramsgate	...	...	38	,,	,,

NAUTICAL MEASURES.

DISTANCE AT SEA is measured in nautical miles. A nautical mile is 6,080 feet, which is the equivalent of 1 minute of longitude measured at the equator.

One tenth of a nautical mile is called a " cable " (=608 feet) and is generally taken as 100 fathoms. In olden times it was about the length of a ship's anchor cable.

A fathom is six feet and is the unit generally used on Admiralty charts for showing the depth of water at any place (at low water).

THE DEPTH OF THE SEA is ascertained either by means of a " lead " lowered to the bottom on a " lead line," or by an " echo sounder," which, in principle, consists in measuring the time the sound of a special bell fitted in the bottom of the ship takes to echo back from the bottom of the sea.

PUBLISHED BY

EAGLE AND QUEEN LINE STEAMERS

(The General Steam Navigation Co., Ltd.)

15, TRINITY SQUARE, LONDON, E.C.3.
Royal 4021.

DAILY SERVICES

(FRIDAYS EXCEPTED)

Whitsun to Mid-September

FROM

LONDON

GRAVESEND, CHATHAM and SHEERNESS

TO

SOUTHEND, MARGATE, RAMSGATE, CLACTON, etc.

FLEET :			
	Passenger Capacity.		Passenger Capacity
M.V. " ROYAL DAFFODIL " 2,093		P.S. " QUEEN OF KENT " 871
P.S. " ROYAL EAGLE " 1,966		P.S. " QUEEN OF THANET " 836
P.S. " GOLDEN EAGLE " 1,336		P.S. " MEDWAY QUEEN " 613
M.V. " CRESTED EAGLE " 408		M.V. " ROCHESTER QUEEN " 415
M.V. " ROYAL SOVEREIGN " 1,783		M.V. " QUEEN OF THE CHANNEL " approx. 1,200 (Building)

J Arthur Dixon postcards produced for the *'Medway Queen Club'*.

Top - *Shore side.*

Centre left - *Forward Saloon.*

Centre right - *Upper Aft Saloon.*

Bottom - *River side.*

6
ISLE OF WIGHT

Isle of Wight businessman Alan Ridett had read of the ship in the Daily Mail newspaper. With his cousin, Colin Ridett, and a third partner, Robert Trapp, he was planning to develop a site between Newport and Cowes as a yacht marina. Without delay they travelled to Rotherhithe to inspect the vessel and within a few days negotiations were complete and with the support of the Medway Queen Trust they became owners of the vessel. Initially they had met resistance but the Director of the Belgian company hearing of the campaign to save the ship agreed to a sale as long as his company did not make a loss. The sale was reported in the Daily Mail on 21st August 1965. The agreed price was £6000 which has an equivalent value by average wages of £190000 in 2012. The scheme was backed by the Dunkirk Veterans Association, the Paddle Steamer Preservation Society and the Medway Queen Trust and the total cost of the enterprise was estimated to be £12000.

Before the ship could be installed in her new home on the island, access had to be made for her through the causeway which separated the mill pond from the river Medina. At first the council withheld planning permission for the scheme but at a special meeting shortly before the ship's arrival permission was granted. The development would comprise PS Medway Queen, sited in the smaller of the two mill ponds, as a club-house and restaurant. The removal of some derelict cottages would allow the construction of a two story building with a workshop and boat storage. The building would also contain a site office and the resident manager's accommodation. The car park would be extended, lock gates placed at the entrance to the larger pond and dredging undertaken to provide access. Slipways and moorings would be constructed and services such as electricity and sewerage disposal provided. Finally the site would be landscaped.

Arrival at Cowes, the pumps in the foreground are Lallow's Jetty. The Classic Boat Museum now occupies the shed behind which was then still part of Saunders Roe. In the background the buildings form the sea-front of East Cowes. PSPS Collection.

Shortly after arrival on the Isle of Wight.

Medway Queen left London on 27 September 1965 under tow to Cowes in the Isle of Wight. She arrived the following day and the event was reported in the Isle of Wight County Press on Saturday 2nd October. The ship was towed by the London Tug Dhulia and they were escorted from the Nab Tower by the minesweeper HMS Droxford – a fitting tribute from the Royal Navy. At Cowes the Dhulia handed over to the motor barges Match and Seaclose, the latter being skippered by a Dunkirk veteran, Mr. C. A. Hocking. There was some concern that a grounded coaster, MV Antelope, might impede the operation but in the event Medway Queen was carefully moved into the mill pond and berthed facing the sea. The operation was supervised by the Newport Harbour Master, Major W. Huxley and one of his staff, Mr. F. Thomas. Both of these gentlemen were also Dunkirk veterans. Once moored, a brief service was held on board, conducted by the Rev Rowton-Lee of Whippingham. The Mayor of Newport, Ald. A. T. Drudge, made a welcome speech and expressed his hopes for the future of the enterprise. Mr. Rowton-Lee presented Alan Ridett with a shell case from HMS Rochester as a memento of the occasion.

Metal theft, especially of non-ferrous metals is not a new phenomenon. Soon after Medway Queen's arrival some of her portholes were stolen. Fortunately the act was seen by a witness who telephoned the police with a description of the thieves' boat. Police Officer Tony Feist relates how he and a colleague, Mervyn Pearson, searched the river in their inflatable dinghy and found the suspect boat near the Cowes "floating bridge". They checked and found the portholes hidden under a canvas sheet in the boat. They withdrew and waited; the boat's crew was arrested when they returned and the portholes restored to their rightful owners.

The club opened for business on Saturday 14th May 1966; annual membership was 3 guineas (£3.15) for one person or 4 guineas (£4.20) for a married couple. Temporary membership, presumably aimed at holiday makers, was 5 shillings (25p) per week. The 2012 equivalents are £92 for personal membership and £124 for a couple.

The opening was a great occasion in the ship's history. The Isle of Wight County Press reported her as "*Gaily painted, dressed overall and with the interior fitted and restored with no loss to the original distinctive character the Medway Queen was a fine sight. Twenty members of the Dunkirk Veterans Association came from all parts of the country for the opening*". After the guests had been

Medway Queen, 4 September 1967. Andrew Munn

welcomed by Mr. Ridett and the club secretary Mr. H. T. Miller, an opening ceremony took place in the engine room. This ceremony was performed by Mr. J. D. Graves who had been her First Lieutenant in 1940. Alan Ridett welcomed the representatives of the Dunkirk Veterans Association, the Paddle Steamer Preservation Society and the Medway Queen Trust and thanked them and all those who had made personal donations for their help in saving the ship. He welcomed the first members of the Medway Queen Club and paid tribute to the efforts of staff and friends in getting everything ready for the day. John Graves stated that there was now a triple role for the Medway Queen in the future. These would be as a pleasure centre, as a meeting place for those who loved the sea and as a memorial to the Dunkirk evacuation. *"Long live the Medway Queen and long may she reign as Queen of the Medina. Full Speed Ahead for ever!"*

At the time of opening the club had some 400 registered members. The Paddle Steamer Preservation Society took out corporate membership of the club so their members were given discounted terms. Details were circulated to all PSPS members, which no doubt contributed to the total. The club was also popular for private functions such as wedding receptions and the restaurant was popular during the day and evenings with locals and holiday makers.

Thomas Russell who had been the ship's cook at Dunkirk visited the club for a special celebration. His record of the event reads *"In 1966, with my brother and our wives, we celebrated my retirement after 40 years of seafaring once more in the Medway Queen. This time I enjoyed a superb meal in leisurely, luxurious style. ……She was now a very beautiful lady indeed, with first class amenities for dining, wining and dancing. She was still a paddle steamer but moored by the shore of the river Medina near Cowes. My galley was a storage cupboard. She carried a brass plaque commemorating her great effort during those historic days, and it was with a deep feeling of pride, when asked to sign her visitor's book, that I saw added carefully in red letters beside my name, Ship's cook during Dunkirk"*

The proprietors produced a selection of promotional material, examples of which have survived. There are many photographs of the ship at all stages of her history but interior shots are scarce because of the capabilities of the average camera. The interior of the ship in her Isle of Wight role is well illustrated by two of the postcards published by J. Arthur Dixon of Newport. There were 4 cards in all, the other two showing the ship's exterior. There was a prospectus and application cards for would-be members. The club was advertised in the island's press and counter top advertising cards were printed.

At some time in the club's history the use of the ship changed subtly with more of a "nightclub" approach. Visitors to a MQPS stand at an Isle of Wight Steam Railway event in September 2007 remembered that the club made full use of the ship's four saloons with a restaurant, music and dancing including live music and discos, a casino and a meeting/function room. It must have been a very successful place as it is fondly remembered by very many people almost 50 years on. The live bands included the "Steamboat" blue grass group and the late Richard Manuel of Bob Dylan's backing group visited from the Isle of Wight Music Festival in 1969 and sat in with the resident musicians Doug Watson and Ernie Hayles. Hank Marvin, of

Peter and Patricia Steele were married in St Paul's Church, Newport on 31st August 1968 and held their reception on board.

Top - *Medway Queen, August 1968. Peter Steele*
Bottom - *Ryde Queen (left) joined Medway Queen in 1970. Andrew Munn*

MQ Club entrance at opening. PSPS collection.

Promotional matchboxes (both sides). PSPS Collection

PS Kingswear Castle (left) with Medway Queen. PSPS Collection.

Shadows fame, also performed at the club on a few occasions. Regular visitors remember that dancing became "more of a challenge" when the tide went out and the ship settled on the mud, heeling gently to one side!

In 1967 Medway Queen had company. The river Dart paddle steamer, Kingswear Castle, was purchased by the Paddle Steamer Preservation Society for £600. She was slipped, surveyed and battened down and then towed to the Isle of Wight where she arrived on 28th August to join the Medway Queen. In 1969 she made her first sailing under PSPS ownership when she was steamed to be filmed for a TV programme 'Bird's Eye View'.

In 1970 a permanent home was found for Kingswear Castle and she was towed down the River to East Cowes ready for the journey to the River Medway. On 16th June 1971 Kingswear Castle departed from Cowes to the River Medway towed by the tug, Daggar. After a stop at Newhaven she arrived on the Medway on 18th June. Full restoration followed and she now plies her trade on the Medway as a popular excursion vessel. Eventually she would be rejoined there by Medway Queen.

In due course the business outgrew the ship's accommodation and a larger vessel was purchased. This was the PS Ryde from the Portsmouth – Ryde ferry service. Another paddler, but significantly newer and larger. She was renamed "Ryde Queen" and moored next to Medway Queen. As HMS Ryde the ship had been used as a minesweeper and was at Dover in the same flotilla as Medway Queen in 1940. Despite that, she does not appear to have been used at Dunkirk. She was later converted for anti-aircraft duties and was used as an HQ ship on D-Day.

The business operated both ships and at one stage accommodation was available on Ryde Queen, advertised as a "boatel". Ryde Queen became a disco aiming at the younger audience whilst Medway Queen concentrated on the slightly older clientele as the restaurant and nightclub. Medway Queen's funnel now sported a black top to match that of the Ryde Queen.

In 1972 when the PSPS held its annual raffle 213 members of the Society managed to sell between them 5,325 tickets which resulted in a gross total of £266.65. The profit was given to the restoration of the Kingswear Castle. Prizes were drawn by Barbara the Medway Queen Club receptionist and included a sailing dinghy, power drill and a Kodak camera.

The Medway Queen Club finally closed in the mid 1970s As often happens with ship-based enterprises the maintenance costs gradually overtook income and she ceased to be viable. She suffered hull damage while being moved out of her berth and became semi-submerged in the river Medina where she began to deteriorate.

The club, now based solely on Ryde Queen carried on. In 1977 Ryde Queen caught fire but was repaired. However, by the late 1980s her popularity was waning and the nightclub was closed completely. Ryde Queen became derelict and abandoned on her mooring. In August 2006 the funnel collapsed and whilst she is still there at the time of writing a successful preservation attempt looks unlikely.

A group of Kent businessmen were interested in returning the steamer to the River Medway for restoration. In 1984 they were ready to proceed and the ship was moved down river to Cowes and loaded on to a submersible salvage pontoon. The operation was recorded in a series of colour slides by the then Harbour Master at Cowes, Captain Henry Wrigley. The ship, on its pontoon was then towed back to Chatham in Kent. Medway Queen was moored just outside the naval dockyard and kept afloat by continuous pumping. This attempt at saving the ship eventually failed through lack of funds. The venture ended up in the hands of the receiver and with no money to pay for the electrical power for the pumps the ship sank once again. The current Medway Queen Preservation Society was formed in 1985 to make yet another attempt at saving this famous old ship, now lying forlornly on the bed of another river.

Right and centre - *Medway Queen's final years on the Island. Dave Cannon*

Below - *Medway Queen leaves Cowes. Henry Wrigley - then Cowes Harbour Master.*

7
PRESERVATION

Medway Queen was home; but with her owners in financial difficulties and the ship sunk alongside St. Mary's wharf, outside Chatham Dockyard, the future was not promising. She ended up in the hands of the Official Receiver lying in the river buffeted by passing ships and almost completely submerged at high water.

There was considerable local interest and in 1985 a local school teacher, Marshall Vine, decided that something must be done. At an event in Chatham Historic Dockyard he rounded up a group of friends and enthusiasts to form a steering committee and preliminary meetings were held in Chatham's historic Brook Pumping Station. A display was arranged at Hempstead Valley shopping complex and a public meeting held on 13th June 1985 at the Rochester Corn Exchange. Over 80 people attended, and the Medway Queen Preservation Society (MQPS) was formed. The ship's legal entanglements were unravelled with the help of local solicitor James Carter, and the Official Receiver who granted access to the ship and agreed a purchase price of £15000.

Work started to raise the money and to prepare for a move under tow. A top-up loan was obtained from the National Westminster Bank with some members acting as guarantors. With the generous help of P&O the "New Medway Steam Packet Company" was revived to own the ship once again, and the purchase was completed in 1987.

The lower decks had two metres of accumulated mud. Volunteers could only work between tides and there was very little equipment. The volunteer "muddies", as they became known, laboured at weekends when the tide permitted. The Dockyard Historical Society loaned a large diesel pump but it wasn't until Gillingham Council made a gulley emptier and crew available for a weekend that any real progress was made in sludge removal.

The society searched the Medway and Thames looking for a suitable working base. There were offers from other towns but the ship belonged on the Medway. Mr. David Dunwell of Bristol Oil and Minerals Ltd., who managed the Kingsnorth industrial site on the Hoo Peninsula, allowed use of his wharf on Damhead Creek for a while. This "while" was to stretch to over twenty years and without this help the project would certainly have failed. Eventually the mud was removed, holes patched and the ship pumped out. Permission to move her was given "on condition that she first remained afloat for 4 tides" to

Under tow to Damhead. Noreen Chambers

MEDWAY QUEEN

Left - *Under tow to Damhead. Noreen Chambers*

Right - *Arrival at Damhead. Iris Painter*

ensure that she was stable. On the 7th November 1987 Medway Queen was taken in tow by the tug Beult II for the eight mile journey to Damhead Creek. At about 10.30am she was eased stern first from her berth and turned to face down river. With the smell of bacon and eggs wafting from the galley and spurred on by cheers from the watching crowd the procession moved off. They were accompanied by the Medway Ports Authority vessel, Medway Otter, which gave assistance in the final stages of the journey. The Port Superintendent kept a close eye on progress to be sure of getting the vessel out of the main channel if a problem developed. The journey was uneventful and Medway Queen arrived at her new base on Damhead Creek. There she was allowed to settle on the mud until more permanent hull repairs could be undertaken.

The society continued to publicise the project locally and beyond, lobbying local businesses, politicians, press and celebrities. From the first few enthusiasts, membership grew to around one thousand, and the society was registered as a charity. The local authorities and press took notice and became enthusiastic supporters; visitors came from far and wide. Once the ship was cleaned and made secure events were held on board and a visitor centre established alongside. The publicity and sales stands travelled all over the South East and beyond. Distant events including Plymouth Navy Days and on board PS Waverley on the river Clyde were included. The society participated in very many radio and TV programmes. In 1996 the ship joined the National Register of Historic Vessels, now the "National Historic Fleet". Gradually the word spread and people from further afield joined in. The fund raising included musical events featuring Clive Dyche's band, 'CRISP'.

David Shepherd, the well known artist and steam enthusiast, spoke at the restoration appeal launch event in Rochester in 1988 and later donated a painting to the fund.

At Damhead Creek the temporary patches were gradually replaced and in 1991 the ship was finally re-floated. The hull still leaked, however, and a constant 24 hour "watch" had to be kept, until an automatic pumping system was installed. Dedicated members undertook this despite going to work bleary eyed the next morning. It is

PRESENTATION EVENING - LAUNCH OF PUBLIC APPEAL

ADMIT
ONE

NO: 9

TICKET
£10.00

Medway Queen Preservation Society

NAME: CLLR. P. HART. DEPUTY MAYOR OF GRAVESHAM.

THE MOORINGS RESTAURANT,
375 HIGH STREET, ROCHESTER, KENT.

24th MARCH 1988 at 7.30p.m.

LOUNGE
SUITS

remembered as a "creepy" experience being alone on the dark ship all night. There was no lighting and the ship creaked and groaned as she moved on the tide. The ship's rumoured ghost was never far from people's thoughts but no sightings were reported. In fact there are no recorded sightings but unexplained footsteps were heard in the starboard engine room gangway and some volunteers and visitors took great pains to avoid the area. Apparently, in the late 1920s, an engineer walked that route and out on to the starboard sponson deck from where he fell or jumped into the sea and was killed instantly by the on coming paddle wheel.

Events and sales stalls are limited in the amounts of money they can raise so the society instigated the "Plate Fund". Donations of £25 or more were recognised by issue of a certificate identifying the hull plate sponsored. The fund was a great success and ran for many years, making a huge contribution towards the rebuild.

A second sales/publicity group started up in the Thames Valley in 1997 greatly increasing the geographical area covered. Teams were visiting schools in the Medway area to raise the society's profile and countless individuals worked to promote the project. These efforts resulted in strengthening the society and raising funds but

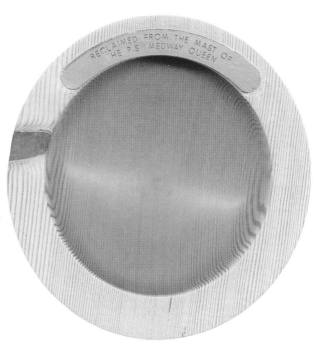

Top - *Souvenier bowl made from the mast of Medway Queen.*

Alongside dockyard wall.

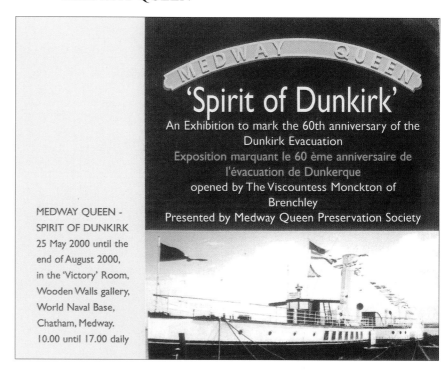

MEDWAY QUEEN - SPIRIT OF DUNKIRK 25 May 2000 until the end of August 2000, in the 'Victory' Room, Wooden Walls gallery, World Naval Base, Chatham, Medway. 10.00 until 17.00 daily

This page - *French membership leaflet, Spirit of Dunkirk brochure and display, May to August 2000.*

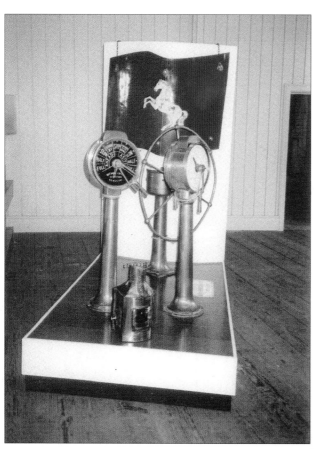

couldn't generate the sums needed for the re-build. They did, however, stand the society in good stead with the National Lottery in later years.

In the year 2000, the 60th anniversary of Dunkirk, a major bi-lingual promotional event, "Spirit of Dunkirk" was held in Chatham Historic Dockyard commemorating Medway Queen's achievements at Dunkirk. The event was supported by a European "Interreg" grant and went on from Chatham to Dunkirk; a precursor of later European cooperation.

The society sales team had started out with various "Medway Queen" promotional souvenirs. Booklets and a VHS video were also produced and sold. Later, customised model railway wagons were added. This unlikely addition to the fundraising armoury worked well. The first wagons were produced in 2003 for 00 gauge and in most years after that new ones were introduced. In 2006 the first N gauge models were added and the scheme continues to this day. In 2011 a DVD was created by Consequential Films and from time to time souvenirs based on unusable material recovered from the ship have been produced. Of these, small bowls created from the old mast were the most successful.

The volunteers worked hard at keeping the ship as presentable as possible and slowing the rate of decay. From time to time a step forward was made. For example in 2002 the funnel was rebuilt by Appledore shipbuilders Ltd of Devon thanks to GMB Union contacts. The Cooperative Society donated £5000 which was used to

Society events on board, including (bottom) the aft saloon decorated for a party to celebrate the ship's 'Birthday'. Marshall Vine

JOURNAL OF THE MEDWAY QUEEN PRESERVATION SOCIETY

FULL AHEAD

ISSUE No. 89 WINTER 2008 £1.50
PATRON: MARIANNA VISCOUNTESS MONCKTON OF BRENCHLEY   To Non Members
PRESIDENT: MARSHALL VINE
VICE-PRESIDENTS: JOHN CHAMBERS, NOREEN CHAMBERS, LEN KNIGHT

www.medwayqueen.co.uk

MQPS is supported by Medway Council, MED Management, Lady Monckton, Admiral Sir Nicholas Hunt GCB, LVO, DL, Dame Vera Lynn DBE, LLD, M.Mus, Sir Mick Jagger, The GMB Union, Ailsa Drydocks Ltd., Mid-Kent College, TT Litho Printers Limited and The CSEU.

REBUILD in BRISTOL

Left - Signing the contract announced in the MQPS magazine. Vernon Stratford

Remaining images - rebuilding at Bristol - 2011/12.
Centre left - Upper forward saloon. Bob Stokes
Centre right - Hydraulic riveting.
Bottom - Hull in dry dock.

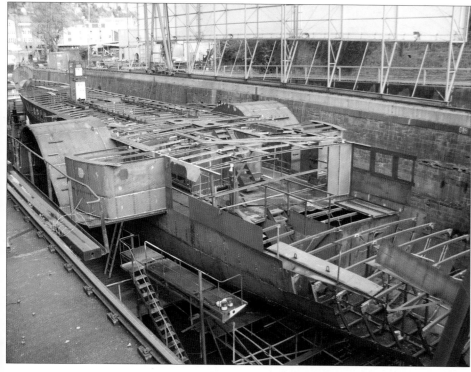

build new paddle boxes. The funnel and paddle boxes then advertised the society in Chatham Historic Dockyard so effectively that passing boaters thought the ship was berthed there.

A massive injection of funding would be needed to save the ship. The National Lottery was the most likely source and successive applications were made. The first was to the Heritage Memorial Fund, in 1998 and then to the Heritage Lottery Fund (HLF) in 2003; prepared by Waverley Excursions Ltd. who had been recommended by HLF. This was for about £6M to cover restoration and the first year in service. The bid was made at the very competitive national level and was unsuccessful. It was swiftly followed by an application to the South East Region of the HLF when their chairman expressed a willingness to help on a Radio Kent news show.

The publicity effort was increasing. A vehicle was donated for use as a mobile display, which gave many years of service in the Medway area, and a large model of the ship was built on a boat trailer for use in carnivals. More large events were added to the repertoire including the 2005 "International Festival of the Sea" in Portsmouth Dockyard. Press coverage spread, encompassing the Isle of Wight where the society began attending occasional events in 2007 and Bristol when the rebuild started there. The project now enjoys comprehensive coverage in the heritage press and elsewhere.

In 2005 a grant of £35000 was made by the HLF towards developing a bid for rebuilding the hull. This last bid was successful and an award of £1.86M was made in June 2006. The re-built hull was to be historically accurate to the 1924 design using riveted construction. Marine consultants advised the society that the existing hull was too fragile to tow or lift onto a pontoon. Therefore the decision was reluctantly taken to dismantle the ship at Damhead Creek and to deliver re-usable material as required for the rebuild by road. Every part of the ship was listed, numbered and photographed as part of the HLF project before dismantling and transportation to Bristol.

A contract was signed with David Abels of Bristol in October 2008 to rebuild the hull. The contract was later transferred to his company; Albion Dockyard Ltd. Abels' yard is based at the Albion Dry Dock near the SS Great Britain in Bristol and was once part of the Charles Hill Shipyard. Work began immediately; preparing working drawings from the originals and starting to build sub assemblies such as bulkheads in the yard's workshops. Another ship occupied the dock and it wasn't until autumn 2009 that construction commenced there.

A members' open Day was held in Bristol on 6th June 2009. On the morning of the event the plans had to be completely revised because the workshop was unexpectedly full of "Medway Queen"! The forward end keel and frame floors had been assembled, ready for lifting into the dock. In that same year the society exhibited at the annual Bristol Harbour Festival for the first time.

The Albion Dockyard used traditional methods and has incorporated as much as possible of the original ship's material. The consultants estimated that the restoration would contain 60-65% original material including the engine. Concessions to modern methods were made, cutting out hull plates using a CNC profiling machine guided by the office computer. Also by hydraulically squeezing the rivets instead of using pneumatic hammers. The hydraulic system is quieter and produces a more repeatable, high quality, joint. The internal joints on bulkheads etc. use round head rivets but the hull plating is "flush rivetted" which requires a countersunk head on the outside. The traditional way of doing this is to insert a hot rivet from the inside and form a countersunk head into the recess on the outside. This technique is being used where access is limited and the hydraulic "iron hands" cannot reach. The hydraulic method has a slow squeezing action which can result in the countersunk end being improperly formed. To avoid this countersunk head rivets are inserted from the outside and a round head is formed on the inside of the hull.

The MQPS and the dockyard have worked closely together and in many cases cooperated on the refurbishment or replacement of parts. The build in Bristol could be viewed via webcams linked to the society's web site (www.medwayqueen.co.uk). At first the build was managed by Mr. Wyn Davies and Fraser Nash Consultants employed by the society and the HLF. From 2011, the society employed a part time project manager while retaining the services of Wyn Davies. Fitting the paddle boxes in late 2011 made a huge difference – the ship became a "paddler" again. The hull plating and promenade deck structure were complete on the forward part of the ship in January 2012 and the refurbished engine was lifted back on board later that year.

In 2010 the society obtained support from the European Development Fund towards the fitting out of the ship as part of the Interreg IVA "Heroes of the Two Seas and Heroes to See" project. This is a partnership of three maritime preservation organisations with MQPS as the lead partner. The aim is to increase cross border cooperation in job creation, tourism and maritime heritage awareness. The other partners are the shipbuilding and training organisation de Steenschuit in Belgian Flanders and the Association Tourville in France.

De Steenschuit are building a replica of the Belgica for the Belgica Society. The Belgica was an Antarctic exploration ship that made several voyages in the late 1800s and early 1900s. The Belgica Society is also looking into the possibility of raising the wreck for display. The ship was used for munitions storage in WWII and was sunk in Norway in 1940. The Tourville Association is building a replica of a 17th century, 84 gun, ship of the line. The design is taken from archive material and information gleaned from wrecks off St. Vaast-la-Houge in Normandy. The ship will be named "The Jean-Bart" after the legendary French captain.

A site was leased from Medway Council on Gillingham Pier early in 2011. Initially for 2 years but extended to cover an approximately 4 year period. An existing building on the site has been refurbished for use as an apprentice training facility. Four instructors and eight apprentices are in place and are working on fitting out the ship. In 2012 their work has mainly been aimed at providing sub assemblies for the hull build in Bristol. Replacements for the massive wooden fenders that protect the paddle boxes have also been built here. The apprentices are students of Mid Kent College and their training is supported by technical expertise from the GMB Union. The main purpose of the Gillingham workshops is to complete restoration of the ship to working order. Machinery needs final assembly and adjustment, panelling and fittings, electrical and plumbing services are required and most of that will have to be purpose built.

The volunteer workforce is still active and shares the Gillingham workshops, primarily in the woodworking section. They have reconditioned many yards of deck planking and built new window frames with safety glass to be fitted to the ship. As the story in this book closes many challenges remain and the saga will continue for a while yet.

Gillingham pier is in reality a masonry faced wharf. The water is tidal with a high range and work was needed to prepare a safe berth for the ship. Fenders have been built to prevent the paddle boxes over riding the walls at high tide. These together with shore side services were required to be completed before the ship's return.

Also on the Gillingham site is the society's office and Visitor Centre. The Visitor Centre was equipped in late 2011 and, in December, hosted a society member's day. For the 2012 tourist season it is regularly open to the public thanks to a small band of hard working volunteers, some of whom remember clearing mud alongside the dockyard wall all those years ago. The Visitor Centre contains a graphic wall telling the story of the ship with other displays of photographs and ephemera. Artefacts waiting to be fitted on the ship are on display and the outside is adorned by an original cast iron "New Medway Steam Packet Company" crest from their Rochester office, donated by the Steam Packet public house.

The question of how to rebuild Medway Queen and how to use her afterwards has caused much debate since the society was founded. Should she cruise as another "Waverley" or be a more modest river trip boat? What about a static restaurant and Dunkirk Museum? All have merit but the final constraints will be financial and dependent on a Maritime and Coastguard Agency license. The current main focus is the rebuild which will not be complete before the end of 2014. By then the financial situation may have changed completely. Fuel price is a dominant factor and those historic ships that operate, and the heritage railways, do not cover their costs; continuing subsidy is needed. The most likely result is a "mobile stately home" which, studies suggest, could pay its way. There would be a heavy voluntary element in staffing with a museum and exhibition space on board and, of course, a good quality restaurant.

The current thinking is that this is less risky than cruising and it will meet the heritage requirements and charitable objectives of the New Medway Steam Packet Company more exactly than rebuilding to revised specifications would have done. The hull has been re-built to the 1924 specification and the ship will be restored to her pre-war condition.

To combine the sentiments of Admiral Ramsay in 1940 and John Graves in 1966:

"Well done Medway Queen."

"Full Speed Ahead for ever!"

SPITHEAD REVIEW

Spithead and the Solent have a tradition of naval reviews by royalty and government officials. Many historic occasions have been marked in this way including coronations, jubilees and the Trafalgar bi-centenary of 2005. In 1953 it would have been an obvious, and very popular, component of the Coronation celebrations for Queen Elizabeth the second. The railway's Special Traffic Arrangements and Carriage Working Notice for the event provide a fascinating insight into the fine detail of planning for the operation. The Coronation took place on Tuesday 2nd June 1953 and the Naval Review at Spithead followed on Monday 15th, with much of the return travel taking place in the early hours of the 16th.

In 1953 there was only one practical way to move the thousands of officials and spectators down to the south coast for such an event – by train. Extra trains would be run to strategic ports nearby, mostly to Southampton Docks and Portsmouth. Naturally the steam-hauled trains, with which we are concerned here, went mostly to Southampton Docks and the electric trains to Portsmouth. The latter included a number of workings by two of the "Brighton Belle" electric Pullman trains from Windsor and Waterloo down to Portsmouth Harbour. The document details 48 special steam trains, mainly from Waterloo or Victoria, in addition to the normal workings which had to suffer minimum disruption, although there

were some cancellations. Many of those normal workings would also have been busy with extra passengers making their way to the Review and in some cases extra coaches were added.

The preparations were meticulous. The possibility of accidents was not overlooked and breakdown cranes in various locations were kept in steam and manned for the duration of the exercise. Nine Elms, Feltham, Stewart's Lane, Bricklayer's Arms, Eastleigh and Fratton cranes were all at readiness. The crane based at Brighton was moved up to Horsham and that from Guildford to Woking. Everything had been done to ensure that assistance could be on site in a minimum time in case of any mishap. Empty carriage workings and storage were planned and the requirements for extra locomotives noted. On the day, empty trains queued on the Windsor line waiting for their turn at Waterloo. Locomotive watering was not forgotten and special instructions were issued for crews arriving at Waterloo with empty trains. On some lines, notably the Mid-Hants route and routes out of Aldershot, the signal box opening hours were extended throughout the night of June 15th. The Ryde-Portsmouth ferry service and all other maritime traffic was banned from noon to 6pm so the 11.38am ferry sailing was the last until until 6.35pm. Alastair Wilson was then a Midshipman, in command of the Admiral's barge of HMS *Illustrious* and spent those six hours

Waterloo early morning on 15 June, three specials await departure. The centre train Platform 10 is train No 1 with 400 passengers for Medway Queen. Bob Ratcliffe

Medway Queen at the review, passing F40. PNS Jhelum, formerly HMIS Narbada.

secured to Ryde Pier. In fact, his boat was the first to move when the Review was over – He had a specific job to collect the Admiral from the *Surprise* which was the temporary Royal Yacht. He got to the *Surprise*, embarked the Admiral, and then, out of the blue, the Queen, Princess Margaret and the Duke of Edinburgh also got into the barge and were taken to the Norwegian Royal Yacht, "Norge". A photograph exists which appears to show the royal party arriving on board the Norge and Medway Queen is prominently in view. Unfortunately it is technically not clear enough for publication.

All special trains carried a headboard with their reference number marked in red. The trains are listed in the Special Traffic Arrangements document and the make-up of each can be found in the Carriage Working Notice that accompanied it. Most used the Southern Region's own rolling stock but train 25 used London Midland Region carriages and train 26 used Eastern Region vehicles. The trains are listed as on hire to shipping companies and other private organisations or to official bodies such as the Admiralty. The document gives train capacities, timings and crucially for me which ships they met up with and where. Many were carrying important guests and sometimes the word "Pullman" appears in the rolling stock descriptions. Others were more mundane but may have met up with equally famous ships. As an example we can take one specific train and use it as an illustration of how the visitors spent their day. The General Steam Navigation Company must have been pretty quick off the mark when bookings opened because they managed to secure trains no. 1 (for *Medway Queen*), no. 2 (for *Royal Sovereign*), no. 5 (for *Royal Daffodil*), and no. 8 (for *Royal Daffodil/Royal Sovereign* combined), a total capacity of 2050 passengers. Most of the steam-hauled trains left from Waterloo or Victoria and ran to Portsmouth or Southampton Old Docks. Exceptions were train number 27 which ran from Victoria to Newhaven, where the passengers transferred to the paddle steamer *Glen Gower*, and train 34 ran to Gosport. Trains 70 and 71 ran from Brookwood for the benefit of the Canadian armed forces and met with the vessel *Eastnore* in Southampton. Train 35 was interesting in that it ran under electric power from Victoria to Chichester where a steam locomotive took over for the run to Fareham. Several trains, including 34 & 35 were carrying naval staff and guests and did not meet specific ships. They watched from shore or were ferried to participating warships. Some returned to London after the Review but before the evening celebrations.

The *Medway Queen* was to take part in the event, not just as an excursion vessel (as she had done in 1937) but as part of the official fleet to be reviewed. Presumably she was selected as a representative of the Merchant Navy and, perhaps, for her part in the Dunkirk evacuation some 13 years before. She would anchor in line, just off the Isle of Wight near Ryde, and wait her turn for the Royal Party to make their way past the long lines of vessels all dressed overall with their signal flags. Her train had a capacity of 400 passengers in 10 coaches. These would have started their journey on the previous day to an assembly point and then formed an empty stock working from Clapham Yard to Waterloo, arriving at 05.50 on the morning of Monday 15th June. It is interesting to note that the principal other traffic mentioned at this time of the morning is milk tank empties, the newspaper trains having all left some time before. A little different to the traffic to be seen now.

Train no. 1 left Waterloo from platform 10, behind locomotive 30856 *Lord St. Vincent*, a Lord Nelson class 4-6-0 locomotive, bound for Southampton Old Docks, at 7am. Trains 5 and 8 followed from the same platform at 7.28am and 8.00am respectively. *Medway Queen's* passengers arrived at berth 47, opposite the famous Ocean Terminal building, at 8.36am with the vessel was timed to depart at 8.55am; not much room for error there.

The passengers had paid 12 guineas (£12-60) each for their tickets for this day out. This represented about a week's wages for the average earner. Tickets were a two-part green ticket over-printed "1" (train number) in red. Tickets for some trains were "coupon" type but there is

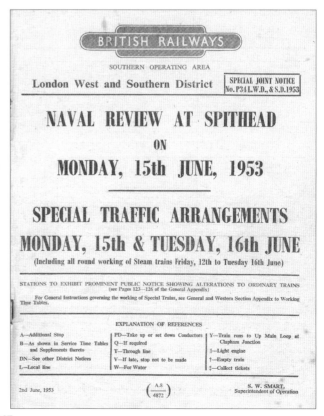

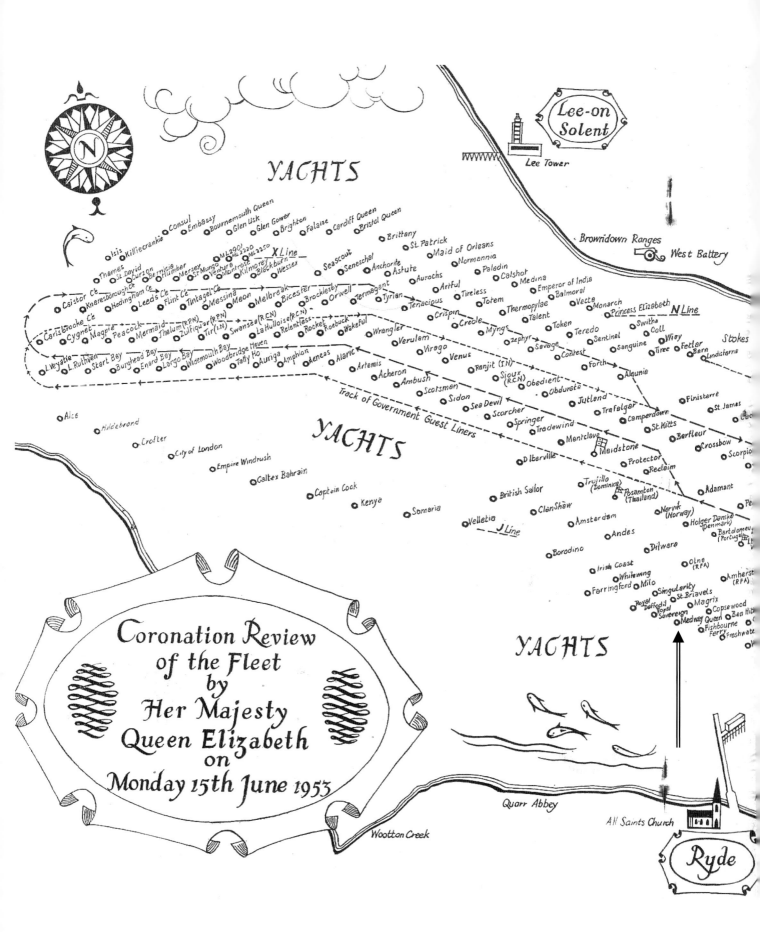

Coronation Review of the Fleet by Her Majesty Queen Elizabeth on Monday 15th June 1953

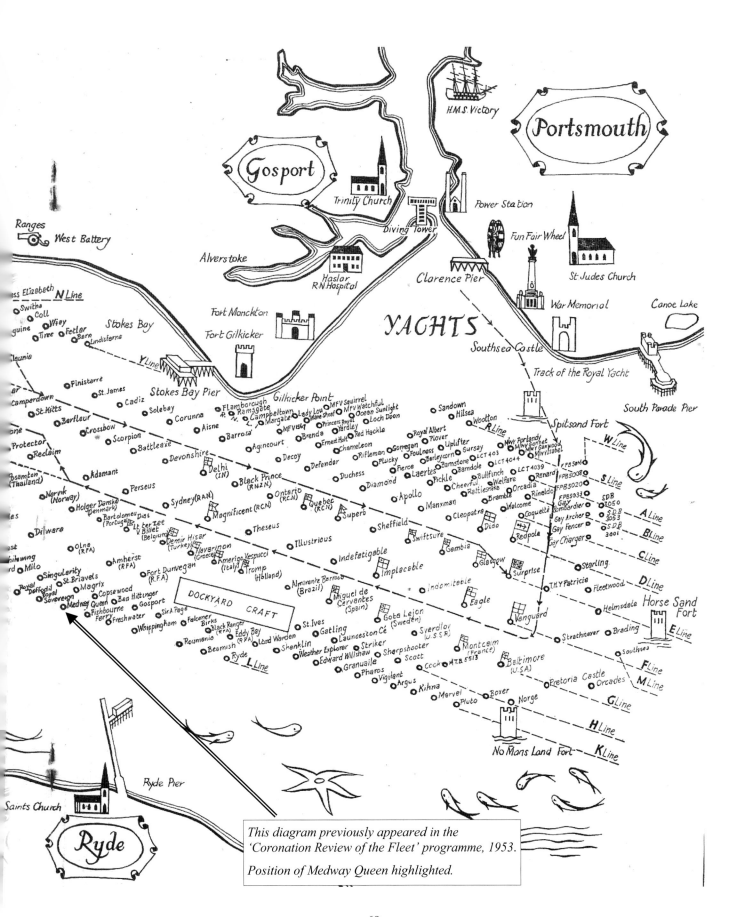

This diagram previously appeared in the 'Coronation Review of the Fleet' programme, 1953.

Position of Medway Queen highlighted.

HMS Surprise acting as the Royal Yacht. Cmdr Alastair Wilson

no indication as to why there was a difference. Return halves were generally valid on normal service trains as well. "Our" train was third class only and meals on the train were not included in the ticket price. So, having spent a week's wages each on their tickets, some of the passengers must have been a little put out when their first view of their ship was the top of a funnel protruding above the dockside. Berth 47 is an ocean liner berth and *Medway Queen*'s 316 tons would be a quite a bit smaller than the usual traffic there: RMS *Queen Mary*, still in service at that time, was 80,000 tons displacement. Most were mollified when told of the vessel's proud history at Dunkirk, however, and with departure imminent and the next ship hovering to take her place the crew would have hurried the passengers on board as quickly as was decently possible.

A minor emergency arose on the trip down Southampton Water when a passenger fell ill. The unfortunate lady was taken ashore by the tug Gladstone which was summoned alongside for that purpose. The rest of the journey was completed without further incident and the ship steamed through the assembled fleet with a naval officer on board to give a commentary on the ships. These included the battleship HMS *Vanguard* and aircraft carriers HMS *Eagle, Illustrious, Implacable, Indefatigable, Indomitable, Perseus, Sydney* (Royal Australian Navy) and *Theseus*. Many foreign navies were represented; including, interestingly, the Italian training ship *Amerigo Vespucci* whose passengers had travelled down on train 38 from Waterloo.

Medway Queen's allotted position was in row "L" just off Ryde Pier. This was not a "front stalls" position by any means but still very much part of the event. The sometimes distant view of proceedings was supplemented by listening to the commentary provided via the BBC "Home Service". Row L included a number of names still well known in paddle steamer circles and the full line was as follows: *Royal Daffodil, Royal Sovereign, Medway Queen, Fishbourne, Freshwater, Whippingham, Roumania, Beamish* and *Ryde*. In plenty of time the ship anchored in her allotted position and with the bar open and a packed lunch included in the price her passengers settled down to wait for the official proceedings to begin. Apparently the packed lunch made a similar impression on some people as had their first sight of the top of the ship's funnel! A cardboard box with a sandwich, apple and biscuit inside was, I am told, less than some had expected for 12 guineas.

The review itself involved a procession of ships carrying the Royal party and a host of dignitaries steaming slowly through the fleet so that the new Queen could inspect the ships. They started from Portsmouth Harbour at 3pm, having travelled down in the Pullman car Phoenix, within a 5-BEL electric set, and were embarked on HMS *Surprise*. At this time the old royal yacht *Victoria and Albert* was no longer in use and the new *Britannia* was not yet available, so a viewing platform had been prepared on board HMS *Surprise,* on 'B' gun-deck, immediately in front of the bridge.. HMS *Surprise* was the C-in-C Mediterranean's dispatch vessel and she had VIP guest accommodation already. HMS *Surprise* was preceded by the Trinity House vessel *Patricia* and followed by a number of ships carrying Admiralty officials and guests. Three liners (*Orcades, Pretoria Castle* and *Strathnaver*) carrying government guests followed but took a slightly different route through part of the fleet. Immediately following the formal review, at 5.35pm, there was a Fleet Air Arm fly-past by aircraft from various naval squadrons. About 300 aircraft in all; in three waves, 45 seconds apart. There was then a pause, during which time Her Majesty dined on board HMS *Vanguard* and at 10.30pm the fleet was illuminated. The firework display was scheduled for 10.40pm with the illuminations turned off at midnight. During the intervals between these activities there was plenty of time for more food (although supplies ran out before the end of the afternoon) and to spend money in the ship's bars. This opportunity was, apparently, exploited to the full by some of the passengers who had to be carried off the ship at the end of the day.

After the fireworks the excursion ships headed back to their designated piers and berths so that the passengers could catch their train home. Naturally this had been carefully planned and time-tabled so that ships would arrive at the right time to meet their own train and the logistics were just as daunting as for the outward journey. For Southampton's berth 47 the schedule was as follows: the *St Patrick* was to dock at 1.55am, with train number 23, organised for the British Railways Executive, departing at 2.38am to arrive in Waterloo at 4.21am and then *Medway Queen* to dock at 2.30am for her train departing at 03-13 to arrive in Waterloo (platform 9) at 4.56am. The return train was the same carriage set as for the outward journey and hauled by a 'King Arthur' class locomotive. One has to wonder if anyone was still awake by that time and what further adventures might have occurred before they actually arrived home. Presumably London's cabbies had a good start to their day!

For the crew of *Medway Queen* it had also been a long day. They were on duty from 7am preparing the ship, raising steam and moving to berth 47 to pick up their passengers at around 8.30am. There followed a long day working the ship and catering to passenger's needs until they went ashore at Southampton early on Tuesday

morning. 7am to 3am the next day might sound like a long working day in itself but the summer season was about to start back at home. So, at 3am, *Medway Queen* left berth 47 and steamed back down Southampton Water. .She headed out to sea at full speed and turned for home. The weather was not ideal and in rough conditions the ship rolled badly, alternately dipping each paddle wheel deep into the water. She eventually headed into the Medway at Sheerness and arrived at Strood at 5pm to be ready for the next day's tourist excursions.

1953 sailing schedule. The sailing from Strood would have been about 9am.

SOURCES and ACKNOWLEDGEMENTS

First; a very big "Thank you" to publisher Kevin Robertson whose sense of humour survived everything I threw at him and to my wife, Jane, who carefully checked through my "engineer's English" and corrected it. Many people have helped me but I must particularly thank Brian Goodhew and George Painter for their patient proof reading and historical checks. George also supplied huge amounts of information and anecdotes for chapters 3 and 5. Thank you too, to Alan Wright and David Abrahams for permission to use pictures taken by their respective Fathers and to everyone who made their own pictures and memories available. I must also thank society archivists Andrew Gladwell of the Paddle Steamer Preservation Society and John Chambers of the MQPS for their help. Mark Ridett, son of Alan, kindly checked the content of the Isle of Wight section. Further information came from MQPS members Noreen Chambers, Marshall Vine, Len Knight and Les Crowder. The current MQPS committee under John Kempton and Brian Burton, and MQPS Sales Officers Roy and June Sedge, have given me all the support and encouragement I needed; thank you all.

During her long life, especially at times of crisis Medway Queen's survival has often relied on small numbers of dedicated people. We owe a huge debt to them all but especially to the activists who battled against the odds to create the MQPS and save the ship. Without them there would be no Medway Queen Preservation Society, no restoration and no ship! Lists of such people compiled some 25 years after the event run a high risk of omissions for which I can only apologise. The early committee (according to MQ News Feb 1988) comprised Marshall Vine, Peter Cooper, Noreen Chambers, Bob Barnes, Ralph and Anne Marsh. They were ably backed up at the time of the tow to Damhead Creek by active volunteers including George Painter, Roy Haigh, Len Knight; Ron Little, Peter Hogwood, Doug Harris, Noel Dollimore, Gill, Barry and Jamie Ellen. Many of these people are still active within the society, although perhaps now less inclined to shovel mud as a hobby!

Publications

Admiral Ramsay's report, published as a supplement in 1947 and available on the London Gazette web site
Coronation Review of the Fleet Official Programme, Commander in Chief Portsmouth, 1953
Dunkirk, Robert Jackson, Cassell, 2002
Full Ahead (the MQPS members' journal) and its predecessor, Medway Queen News
His Majesty's Minesweepers, HMSO, 1943
Mainly in Minesweepers, Charles McAra, R J Leach and Co, 1991
Medway Queen, A Paddle steamer that went to war, J. B. Millar, PSPS, 1974
          Includes Thomas Russell and J D Graves accounts of Dunkirk
Medway Queen, the survivor, MQPS
Pillar of Fire, Ronald Atkin, Birlinn Ltd., 2000
Return from Dunkirk Railways to the rescue, Peter Tatlow, Oakwood Press, 2010
River Medway Pleasure Steamers, Andrew Gladwell, Amberley Publishing Plc, 2010
Special Train Working Notices, British Railways Southern Region, 1953
Special Train Working Notices, Southern Railway, 1937

Other sources

Archives and Local Studies Centre, London Borough of Barking and Dagenham
Dover Castle, wartime tunnels including the "Dynamo" operations room
Essex Record Office
Explosion, Museum of Naval Firepower, Gosport
Isle of Wight County press
Kent History and Library Centre, Maidstone
Library of the National Museum of the Royal Navy, Portsmouth
National Archives, Kew
Plans and photos archive, National Maritime Museum, Woolwich

Various web sites – I have a possibly irrational suspicion of the data available on the web although most of it is undoubtedly genuine and accurate. As far as is possible, information from these and other sources has been cross checked. Wikipaedia and www.naval-history.net especially useful.

Chapter 8, "Spithead Review", has been adapted from Southern Way 15 (July 2011) with the permission of Kevin Robertson. That depended on information supplied by Mr. Bob Ratcliffe who was on the "Medway Queen" train and to Mr. Brian Goodhew who was working on the ship on that day and who is now PR Officer for the Medway Queen Preservation Society. Also Cmdr. Alistair Wilson R.N. Ret'd who was a Midshipman commanding an Admiral's barge at the event.